AF605928

Giovanni Boccaccio

RIME: The Complete Lyric Poetry

For centuries, the sonnet tradition has captivated European writers, beginning with Giacomo da Lentini and flourishing in the hands of Dante and Petrarch. Yet while Dante's and Petrarch's lyric poetry has long been available to English readers through numerous translations, the complete work of Giovanni Boccaccio – the third of Italy's Three Crowns – remains largely inaccessible in English, despite his towering influence.

The *RIME* bridges this gap by presenting the first complete English translation of Boccaccio's poetry alongside the original Italian text. Based on Antonio Lanza's modern edition, this translation brings to life Boccaccio's mastery of the sonnet form and lyrical voice, shedding new light on his poetic achievements.

With an insightful introduction and extensive notes, this book serves as a vital resource for students and scholars of Italian literature. A long-overdue addition to the canon of translated Italian literature, this edition ensures that Boccaccio's lyrical brilliance can finally be appreciated in English.

RICHARD LANSING is a professor emeritus of Italian and comparative literature at Brandeis University.

AKASH KUMAR is an assistant professor of Italian studies at the University of California, Berkeley.

THE LORENZO DA PONTE ITALIAN LIBRARY

Toronto Buffalo London
utppublishing.com
Printed in Canada

ISBN 978-1-4875-6513-8 (cloth)
ISBN 978-1-4875-6514-5 (paper)
ISBN 978-1-4875-6516-9 (EPUB)
ISBN 978-1-4875-6515-2 (PDF)

Library and Archives Canada Cataloguing in Publication

Title: Rime : the complete lyric poetry / Giovanni Boccaccio ; translation and notes by Richard Lansing ; introduction by Akash Kumar.
Other titles: Rime. English
Names: Boccaccio, Giovanni, 1313–1375, author. | Lansing, Richard H., translator. | Kumar, Akash, 1984– writer of introduction. | Translation of: Boccaccio, Giovanni, 1313–1375. Rime. Italian. (Lanza)
Series: Lorenzo da Ponte Italian library.
Description: Series statement: The Lorenzo da Ponte Italian library | Includes bibliographical references and index. | English translation based on the Italian text edited by Antonio Lanza.
Identifiers: Canadiana (print) 20250178168 | Canadiana (ebook) 20250180375 | ISBN 9781487565138 (hardcover) | ISBN 9781487565145 (softcover) | ISBN 9781487565152 (PDF) | ISBN 9781487565169 (EPUB)
Subjects: LCGFT: Lyric poetry. | LCGFT: Poetry.
Classification: LCC PQ4272.E5 R56 2025 | DDC 851/.1–dc23

Cover design: Louise OFarrell
Cover and title page image: Bodleian Library MS. Holkham misc. 49, fol. 80v.
Ornament: iStock ID: 163818088 Eoseye.

This volume is published under the aegis and the financial assistance of Agincourt Press Ltd. and Casa Italiana Zerilli – Marimó of New York University.

We wish to acknowledge the land on which the University of Toronto Press operates. This land is the traditional territory of the Wendat, the Anishnaabeg, the Haudenosaunee, the Métis, and the Mississaugas of the Credit First Nation.

University of Toronto Press acknowledges the financial support of the Government of Canada, the Canada Council for the Arts, and the Ontario Arts Council, an agency of the Government of Ontario, for its publishing activities.

Canada Council for the Arts
Conseil des Arts du Canada

Funded by the Government of Canada
Financé par le gouvernement du Canada
Canada

THE LORENZO DA PONTE ITALIAN LIBRARY

Giovanni Boccaccio

RIME

The Complete Lyric Poetry

Translation and Notes by Richard Lansing

Introduction by Akash Kumar

UNIVERSITY OF TORONTO PRESS
Toronto Buffalo London

For Johanna

and

in memory of
Ann and Janet

Contents

Preface

The text for this verse translation of Boccaccio's *Rime* is taken from the edition prepared by Antonio Lanza and published in 2010 by Aracne (Rome). His edition contains lyrics (*rime*) considered authentic by all critics, a second group of lyrics deemed of questionable authorship by many critics (*rime dubbie*), and a third set of lyrics that Lanza regards as spurious (*rime spurie*). In keeping with his view that this last group of lyrics cannot be assigned to Boccaccio with any certainty, I have omitted them from consideration, with the exception of four lyrics. I have included those *rime* because, except for Lanza, almost all critics regard them as authentic, among them Vittore Branca and Roberto Leporatti, both of whom have published editions of Boccaccio's corpus of lyrics, as well as a number of American scholars whose publications make reference to them. These lyrics, all sonnets, constitute an *apologia* addressed to Boccaccio's adversaries for his supposed disparagement of Dante's *Commedia* by having delivered readings of its cantos to the general public of Florence, an audience his detractors considered devoid of intellectual competence and cultural refinement. These *rime* are grouped separately.

I have made no changes to the original Italian text except to alter the format of the poems' numbering from Roman to Arabic for the reader's benefit.

In a note to his translation of Dante's *Commedia*, Charles S. Singleton remarks that "the best 'introduction' given here ... is no *Introduction* at all. Let the reader face the poem directly."[1] He consequently placed his introduction after the text and translation of the *Inferno*, at the very end of the volume. By the same token, it might be said that the best explanation regarding the attitude of, or decisions made by, the translator about the method used requires no explanation since it is a given that a translator always seeks to provide a faithful rendering of the original text in a language easily accessible to readers. A translator must always be concerned with the meaning of a poem's expression and the signification of its words and phrases as parts of the whole. This is more difficult in verse than in prose translation because of strictures imposed by the choice of metre, verse length, and stanzaic form. A major challenge – one might even say the primary challenge – is deciding whether to carry over the literal sense of the words in the original, or the meaning of those words. I know of no formula that might usefully be followed to guide the translator in making a choice between the two approaches: each instance requires its own solution. But if a literal rendering does not, or is unable to, convey the actual meaning of the original, it has no true purpose.

For this reason, I have rejected replicating the rhyme scheme of the original, or, for that matter, using rhyme at all. To use it would inevitably distort a poem's most important quality: its meaning on all levels. The format of my translation is traditional: iambic pentameter for hendecasyllables, iambic trimeter for *settenari*, with the same stanza format as in the original. This translation aims to be literal in so far as possible within the strictures of a verse format. A translation of a poem should read like a poem in its own right. It should display a natural flow of words, common syntax, and a normal sequence of thoughts. In sum, it should not only look like a poem but also read and sound like a poem.

Together with Dante and Petrarch, Boccaccio formed the Italian vernacular that would be become the Italian language used today. While Boccaccio as a practitioner of poetry was less inventive than either Dante or Petrarch and owed much to the stilnovist tradition or to an earlier period of poetry, his *rime* are characterized by an elegance of expression and a thematic coherence that often raise them well above the level of the mundane. Many of the *rime* are unusually well crafted and reveal a degree of originality, portraying an amatory experience neither stilnovistic nor Petrarchan in spirit. As in the *Decameron*, Boccaccio embraces in his lyrics the temporal world as his poetic domain.

---

1 Dante Alighieri, *The Divine Comedy*, ed. Charles S. Singleton (Princeton, NJ: Princeton University Press, 1970), 1:371. All English translations of Dante's *Commedia* are taken from this edition unless otherwise indicated.

Acknowledgments

It is a pleasure to express my gratitude to those who have contributed to this translation. Maria Luisa Ardizzone gave important advice and made many suggestions at the onset of the project, and Christopher Kleinhenz provided numerous comments regarding the poems towards the end of Boccaccio's collection. I am grateful to Antonio Lanza for his extensive and invaluable advice on questions of meaning in the *rime*, and especially to Akash Kumar, who wrote the introduction to this volume and to whom I am indebted for his many perceptive remarks along the way. I thank Teodolinda Barolini for her unwavering support and encouragement, and Victoria Kirkham for discussions regarding Boccaccio's work in general. Finally, I am indebted to Joan Ferrante, who first introduced me to Boccaccio, and to Robert Durling for teaching me the importance of translating with precision and clarity.

RIME

Introduction

Giovanni Boccaccio is not typically thought of as a poet. In the literary tradition celebrating the founding fathers of Italian literature as the "tre corone," the three crowns of literary excellence, genre serves as a primary distinguishing factor in determining the categorical uniqueness of each of the fourteenth-century founders. Dante is renowned for his vernacular epic, the *Commedia*; Petrarch for the lyric poetry gathered and given order in his *Rerum vulgarium fragmenta*; and Boccaccio for the prose narrative of his *Decameron*, a collection of short stories written in the wake of the bubonic plague of 1348. Yet even the reader of the *Decameron* is mindful of Boccaccio as poet since at the conclusion of each day of storytelling, a member of the *brigata* sings a love song, which is inscribed in the text as a poem. What is far less known is that Boccaccio wrote a significant number of poems in the vernacular, a fact even more less known to the English-speaking world owing to the fact that his lyric poems have never been translated into English in their entirety. While Boccaccio's other extended poetic works, such as the *Caccia di Diana* (c. 1334), the *Amorosa visione* (c. 1343), and the *Ninfale fiesolano* (c. 1344), have received greater attention and more recent translation efforts, such is not the case for Boccaccio's occasional lyric poetry.

Boccaccio's *rime* comprise 127 poems of certain attribution and an additional nineteen whose authorship remains in question. They are predominantly sonnets, though other genres such as the *canzone*, the *sirventese*, the madrigal, and the *ballata* also make appearances. Some of his early lyrics likely predate his first formal work, the *Caccia di Diana* (Diana's hunt), and his lyric laments of a spiritual, Petrarchan nature extend well into his old age. In fact, Boccaccio writes a sonnet mourning the death of Petrarch in 1374, just a year before his own death. Contrary to Petrarch's obsessive ordering of his poetry into the form that we now think of as a songbook, or *canzoniere*, it seems clear that Boccaccio never intended to collect and organize his poetry in such a way. Some even believe that he intended his poems to be burned when he died, not unlike the story of Virgil leaving instructions to have his *Aeneid* burned after his death.

Boccaccio's lack of self-regard and clear intent is evident in the history of the transmission of the surviving body of poetry. A wide dispersion of Boccaccio's poetry, across more than 100 manuscripts of the fifteenth and sixteenth centuries, accounts for the 127 poems that can be firmly attributed to him. The principal source of transmission is the *Raccolta Bartoliniana*, a sixteenth-century compilation that includes 100 sonnets by Boccaccio. However, Domenico De Robertis's 1984 essay, Antonio Lanza's 2010 edition, and Roberto Leporatti's 2013 critical edition have all emphasized the importance of valuing the various scattered sources that fill out what remains of Boccaccio's poetic output.[1] Indeed, Leporatti divides his edition into sections for each distinct manuscript source, insisting that readers and scholars reckon with the full range of the material record.

Boccaccio's poetry was first edited in 1802 by Giovanni Battista Baldelli Boni.[2] A century later, in 1914, Aldo Francesco Massera produced the first authoritative modern edition.[3] Focusing on the *Raccolta Bartoliniana* as the most important source for the corpus, Massera sought to arrange the poems to recreate a sort of sentimental journey through the life of the artist. The eminent Boccaccio scholar Vittore Branca published his first edition of the *Rime* in 1939, with later revised editions in 1958 and 1992.[4] Branca saw in the lyric corpus something to be appreciated in Boccaccio's artistic experiments that related, certainly, to the writer's other works in select instances, but also as a work that stood on its own. In the key of nineteenth- and early twentieth-century criticism, he pointedly argued against reading the poems as the precious testimony of the author's life, as represented most clearly in Massera's artificial ordering.

The collection's lack of order and constant shifting from the style of one school of poetry to another should not, however, be taken as a flaw or a lack of originality on the part of the author. There are certainly

1 Domenico De Robertis, "A norma di stemma (per il testo delle rime di Boccaccio)," *Studi di filologia italiana* 42 (1984): 109–49; Antonio Lanza, ed., *Le Rime*, by Giovanni Boccaccio (Rome: Aracne, 2010); Roberto Leporatti, ed., *Rime*, by Giovanni Boccaccio (Florence: SISMEL Edizioni del Galluzzo, 2013).

2 Giovanni Battista Baldelli Boni, ed., *Rime di Messer Giovanni Boccacci* (Livorno: Tommaso Masi & Co., 1802).

3 Aldo Francesco Massera, ed., *La Caccia di Diana e Le Rime*, by Giovanni Boccaccio (Turin: UTET, 1914).

4 Vittore Branca, ed., *Rime*, by Giovanni Boccaccio, vol. 5.1 of *Tutte le opere di Giovanni Boccaccio* (Milan: Mondadori, 1992).

times when Boccaccio's *rime* seem artificially derivative, if not awkwardly imitative in nature. Indeed, his poetry has been marginalized and relegated to the realm of curiosity precisely because of its history of critical disregard. Editors of his verse have on occasion harshly criticized even the quality of composition of specific lyrics. Antonio Lanza, for example, characterizes sonnet 62 as "forced and less than successful" and sonnet 2 as "lacking even a shred of originality."[5]

Reading through Boccaccio's lyric poetry provides a way of connecting across various phases and movements of the Italian lyric tradition, from thirteenth-century poets such as Guido Guinizzelli and Cecco Angiolieri, to the new style (*stil novo*) of Dante as well as to his lyric experiments of the *rime petrose*, to the sweet refinement of Cino da Pistoia (with whom Boccaccio studied law in Naples), and finally to the influence of Petrarch. Antonio Lanza's 2010 edition, which serves as the basis of this translation, privileges such a mode of reading through the various stylistic and thematic phases of Boccaccio's decades of poetic production. This does not require setting aside the issue of material transmission that Leporatti uses as his primary means to organize his recent edition. Rather, Lanza's choice emphasizes a mode of reading that values the markedly different stages of Boccaccio's poetic itinerary and urges one to see how he connects to, departs from, and fuses together the various voices of the lyric tradition before him.

Nevertheless Boccaccio's subtle reworking and combining of sources reveals startling moments of transformation. Roberto Fedi rightly claims that "Boccaccio is seeking an original, or at least autonomous path within the forest of amorous lyric that is contemporary or immediately prior to him."[6] In sonnet 103, *The sky was clear and calm, adorned with stars*, Boccaccio depicts, for example, a scene that finds the lover looking at the night sky when a flame blazing across it, the soul of Fiammetta, says that whoever wants to be with her must be kind, obedient, and humble. Boccaccio often plays on the name of his lady Fiammetta, "little flame," her *senhal*, her secret code name, as Petrarch does with Laura. This sonnet constitutes a song of mourning for the dead beloved as well as hope for a reunion in the beyond. Boccaccio's chosen words, however, indicate that something has shifted. The flame says, "He who desires to be with me / must be kindhearted and obedient / and clothed in humbleness" (10–12). Reading these words, especially the turn of phrase "d'umiltà

5 My translation. "artificioso e poco riuscito"; "senza la benchè minima originalità." Lanza, *Le Rime*, 124, 7.

6 Roberto Fedi, "Pathways through the Lyric Forest (*Rime*)," in *Boccaccio: A Critical Guide to the Complete Works*, ed. Victoria Kirkham, Michael Sherberg, and Janet Levarie Smarr (Chicago: University of Chicago Press, 2013), 289.

vestito" (clothed in humbleness), it is impossible not to think of Dante's sonnet *Tanto gentile,* that perfect distillation of Dante's new style that makes of his lady a miracle on earth who has the power of ennobling others by her very presence. In that sonnet, which will come to have a place of prime importance in the *Vita nova,* it is the lady who is "benignamente d'umiltà vestuta" (she moves benignly, clothed in humbleness) as she silences onlookers and provokes the most exquisite sigh of desire.[7] In Boccaccio's sonnet, however, it is the lover who must be "d'umiltà vestito" in order to be worthy of joining his beloved among the happy souls above. Such an adaptation of Dante's language is by no means benign; rather, it urges one to think about gender roles and obligations, as the male lover is humbled in the face of a lady who streaks across the sky in the form of a flame.

Readers of the *Decameron* are certainly familiar with such explicit reworkings of Dante's language and tropes from across the full range of the *Commedia* as well as role reversals and transgressive boundary crossings. Seeing such continuities in Boccaccio's lyric prompts us both to re-examine the work of his poetic predecessors through this lens and to appreciate the unique ways in which he engages with the tradition before him. The imagery of the first eight verses of sonnet 103 depicting an idyllic scene of a night sky disrupted by the flame of light exemplifies Boccaccio's lyric signature, which critics have termed late Gothic, embodying the artistic style of the late fourteenth and early fifeenth centuries that featured luminous figures, highly stylized natural settings, and at times a pronounced lack of religious inspiration. Even in this instance it is only in the final six verses that the sonnet promises a reunion with the beloved in paradise in the way that Petrarch or Dante might do, and it gives no particular emphasis to the spiritual other than the final verse that defines paradise as "the sacred realm of happy souls" (14).

In a number of remarkable sonnets, Boccaccio's luminous depiction of an idyllic scene, or *locus amoenus,* specifically evokes the ambiance of the Neapolitan seaside, a place with which he had long been familiar. In 1327, at the age of thirteen, he had left Florence for Naples, where he first worked as an apprentice to a banking house before taking up his studies, not returning to Florence until 1341. This period proved to have a great influence on his artistic life, and poems evoking the Neapolitan setting strongly distinguish Boccaccio's verse from others of this period. Scholars ranging from Rosario Ferreri to Ilaria Tufano have agreed that

---

7 *Vita nova* 26.6. For the English translation, see Dante Alighieri, *Vita Nuova,* trans. Virginia Jewiss (New York: Penguin, 2022). All English translations of the *Vita nova* are taken from this edition.

these particular poems, known as the Baia sequence for their focus on the seashore life of that small community, make idiosyncratic use of the classical tradition, from Ovid to perhaps even Propertius.[8]

A marine setting figures in other lyrics as well. Sonnet 54, *Barefoot, scantly dressed, her hair in braids,* is considered by many to be perhaps Boccaccio's finest and most original lyric. It depicts a scene of sensuality within the natural setting of seashore, dwelling on the alluring body of the beloved, who, barely clothed, climbs over rocks collecting seashells with her companions. Even the breaking waves, it seems, desire to be with her: "And as if piling on themselves, the waves, / submerging her white feet in little swirls, / propelled themselves ahead while murmuring / and then receded many times in turn" (5–8). Painstakingly detailing the soft and repeated breaking of the waves on his beloved's fair feet, Boccaccio crafts a remarkably immersive lyric experience. When the beloved raises her skirt to prevent it from becoming wet, inadvertently revealing her thigh, the poet becomes a voyeur wishing only to see her skirt raised even higher. Importantly, there is not a single trace of religious authority in this poem, nor any indication of shame or torment on the part of the poet.

The seashore was for Boccaccio also a locus of moral degeneracy. A series of sonnets (40–9) depicting experiences at the vacation site of Baia near Naples portrays it both as a place of beauty, festivity, and song and also, in the same breath, as a place of licentiousness that threatens to corrupt Fiammetta's virtue. In sonnet 47, *May your name perish, Baia, with your town,* Boccaccio rails against the community, wishing that its name might disappear, its cultivated fields turn into wild forests, and its fountain run with poison. In so imagining that his lady, or indeed any lady, could be corrupted by such a place of seasonal celebration, Boccaccio departs from the conventions of the lyric tradition that idealize the beloved with unequivocal praise and suppress any form of a realistic social milieu.

Boccaccio's *rime* do not treat the theme of love exclusively. In sonnet 108, the poet laments that "All virtue's fled, what is of value dead / which made Italia lady of the world" (1–2). Similar poems decry the decadence of his age, which he says would "call a beast whoever turned / away from following the erudite / in wasting time at building up their wealth" (110.12–14), and which no longer prizes the likes of a Plato or a Virgil. In sonnet 122, Boccaccio reveals his late Gothic sensibility in a poem addressed to the Virgin Mary, who is praised for her humility above all

8 See Rosario Ferreri, "Ovidio e *Le Rime* di G. Boccaccio," *Forum Italicum* 8, no. 1 (1974): 46–55, https://doi.org/10.1177/001458587400800103; Ilaria Tufano, *"Quel dolce canto": Letture tematiche delle "Rime" di Boccaccio* (Florence: Cesati, 2006), esp. 103–5.

the traditional tropes of love poetry: "No golden tress, no splendour of the eyes, / no regal finery, no graciousness" (1–2). In naming and negating such qualities, Boccaccio draws on both Dante's fusing of courtly love with theology as well as Petrarch's Augustinian rejection of the earthly in favour of the purely spiritual.

One of the most compelling moments in Boccaccio's corpus that has little to do with love comes in his participation in a *tenzone*, an exchange of sonnets prompted by the proposing of a question or problem to which others are asked to respond in the same poetic form. Two exchanges in which Boccaccio participated are extant: one is a debate on whether it is preferable to choose a virgin or a widow for a wife; the other, much more extended debate engages questions regarding the influence of free will, astral determinism, natural disasters, and divine justice. This second *tenzone*, prompted by a poet from Forlì by the name of Cecco di Miletto de' Rossi, brings together five poets and includes among them Petrarch. Cecco argues that while everyone is powerless against the workings of nature and subject to divine justice, the stars do not determine human actions. The responses of the other poets lean towards an emphasis on human inadequacy, whether by means of possessing the power to change the motion of the heavens or by interpretating the signs of nature.

Boccaccio's own response, sonnet 82e, distinguishes itself for its emphasis on the virtues of mercy and understanding. He reasons that Adam and the ancient Israelites, though closer to perfection because closer in historical time to God, still erred in spite of seeing "a thousand miracles" (7). As a consequence, he and his contemporaries should not, he argues, be troubled by their own flaws, and, moreover, God would have compassion on their plight: "while eclipses of the sun, or clouds / being ruptured, are cause for a little fear, / whoever feels it does not mind it much. // The one who died to end our servitude / will show us mercy on our trying journey" (12–16). Boccaccio's message of hope strikes a chord, especially if one considers that this poetic exchange is datable to 1348, the year that the bubonic plague pandemic decimated the population of Florence. In his emphasis on mercy in this time of crisis, one can almost detect the first line of the *Decameron*, "Umana cosa è aver compassione degli afflitti" (It is a human quality to show compassion for those who suffer).[9]

One moment in Boccaccio's lyrics, related in sonnets 125 and 126, stands out for being based on an extraordinary factual event. Defending himself against critiques of his art and his person, Boccaccio rebukes an unnamed individual (most likely the Gran Siniscalco Niccolò Acciaiuoli)

9 My translation.

who criticized him for immoral conduct: "You run me through, and I'm not made of steel: / and if my wounds compel me to respond / by giving you the beating you deserve, / I think you'll find you've stirred a hornet's nest" (125.1–4). These two sonnets expose the sordid tale of an individual who conceives an illegitimate child with a servant and then commits infanticide to avoid the resulting scandal. Boccaccio does not hold back in excoriating this individual as a "wicked priest" (126.12) who fathered a child at an advanced age and drowned it in a latrine.

While these two lyrics have no parallel in Boccaccio's corpus for their naked realism, in a set of four sonnets gathered under the title "Boccaccio's Response to His Adversaries," Boccaccio puts aside the world of amatory experience to push back against ad hominem criticism that his public lectures on Dante's *Commedia* did harm by exposing the sublime truths of the poem to the vulgar masses. These poems ask us to consider the relationship between intellectuals, government, and the burgeoning vernacular culture of fourteenth-century Florence. Though Boccaccio acknowledges that he may have erred and details the great suffering that he has endured due to the criticism he has received, he also berates his unnamed adversaries for having gone too far in their attacks and puts the blame on the public for their inability to understand.

Many other poems in Boccaccio's *rime* also reach beyond the borders of the closed world of the courtly love lyric. Sonnet 75, *Hippocrates, Avicenna, or Galen,* plays on cultural alterity and prestige in listing a series of individuals, objects, and forces that prove inadequate in curing the poet of the rabid spirit of love that resides in his breast. The opening gathers a multicultural canon of medical authorities: the Greek Hippocrates, the Persian Avicenna, and the Roman Galen. This ordering also happens to precisely replicate Dante's in *Inferno* 4.143, which places these medical authorities near the end of the catalogue of non-Christian figures of excellence inhabiting Limbo. Such borrowing from Dante is hardly surprising from the likes of Boccaccio, one of his most ardent admirers and readers. But it can encourage one to consider how Boccaccio reads such moments of Mediterranean connectivity and redeploys them to his own ends. In this particular case, we can think about the medical canon, the institutionalizing of medical knowledge that includes Avicenna. In the introduction to Day 1 of the *Decameron,* where Boccaccio dwells on how people of all ages who would be deemed healthy by the greatest medical authorities could die on the very same day, the name of Avicenna is dropped and Aesculapius is added.[10] Yet, in *Decameron* 8.9, the names of

10 Giovanni Boccaccio, *Decameron,* ed. Vittore Branca (Turin: Einaudi, 2004), 1:47.

Hippocrates and Avicenna are playfully invoked by Bruno as a means of tricking the physician Maestro Simone.[11]

Sonnet 75 moves from medical authorities to precious stones, then to medicinal plants, religious texts, atmospheric phenomena, the occult ("magicians, necromancers, fortune tellers"; 6), non-Christians, and, finally, universal human misery in the form of poverty and pain. A certain through line emerges from this catalogue that focuses on the exotic, from Avicenna to "a Tartar, or a Jew or Saracen" (7), and that asks the reader to perceive the connected world through the eyes of the forlorn lover. It points to Boccaccio's interest in how such things and people interact with one another in a social community. The exotic is thus not only juxtaposed with the familiar and religiously orthodox ("the psalms, the gospels, speeches"; 4), but it also becomes part of the same cultural continuum. This sonnet thus serves as a lens through which to look back on *Inferno* 4 and its challenge to the spirit of religious exclusion as well as outwardly to Mediterranean currents within the *Decameron*, as illustrated by the novella 1.3, for example, which promotes a remarkable vision of religious tolerance in the tale of the friendship between the Jew Melchisedech and Egyptian Sultan Saladin.

Though translations of a few of Boccaccio's poems can be found in anthologies and critical companions, there has never been a complete translation of Boccaccio's lyric poetry in English. Richard Lansing has here produced versions of the poems that wonderfully balance the constraints of fidelity to the text, readability, and the music of poetry. His work provides access to a corpus of literature that should be better integrated into anglophone Boccaccio scholarship, and it will serve as an invaluable resource for those interested in having a more complete picture of Giovanni Boccaccio as a writer.[12] Boccaccio's lyrics provide great

11 My thanks to Pier Mattia Tommasino (Columbia University) for our discussion of this sonnet and its implications. For more on the vernacularizing of non-Western names between Dante and Boccaccio, see Akash Kumar, "Walls of Inclusivity: Dante's *Divine Comedy* and World Literature," in *A Companion to World Literature*, ed. Ken Seigneurie (West Sussex: John Wiley & Sons, 2020), https://doi.org/10.1002/9781118635193.ctwl0057.

12 Recent publications seeking to integrate Boccaccio's lyric into broader considerations of his work include Alison Cornish, *Vernacular Translation in Dante's Italy: Illiterate Literature* (Cambridge: Cambridge University Press, 2010), https://doi.org/10.1017/CBO9780511734762; James C. Kriesel, *Boccaccio's Corpus: Allegory, Ethics, and Vernacularity* (Notre Dame, IN: University of Notre Dame Press, 2018), https://doi.org/10.2307/j.ctvpj7f5b; and Elsa Filosa, *Boccaccio's Florence: Politics and People in His Life and Work* (Toronto: University of Toronto Press, 2022), https://doi.org/10.3138/9781487532727.

insight into his other works; they also provide a window on the early formation of the canon of Italian poetry and on the turn to Petrarchism that would dominate the lyric tradition for centuries in Italy and Europe as well. Paola Vecchi Galli perceives in Boccaccio's poetic range an eclecticism that reflects late fourteenth-century tastes before a more strict adherence to Petrarch would eventually take hold.[13] Indeed, Boccaccio was a plurilingual poet who experimented widely with different genres and tropes, combining and modifying them to create, as it were, his own music. He may have ultimately gone in the direction of Petrarchan *monolinguismo,* but the present translations should provoke in readers new ways of understanding Boccaccio and Italian Duecento and Trecento poetry, not to say Petrarch himself.

In the final year of his own life, Boccaccio wrote sonnet 127, *You have ascended now, my dearest lord,* mourning the death of Petrarch in 1374. This poem, supplicating and deferential in tone, expresses reverence for Petrarch as his "dearest lord" (1), entreating Petrarch to bring Boccaccio into heaven along with him: "Ah, if you loved me in the wayward world, / draw me behind you, where I happily / will see the one who first enamoured me!" (12–14). Yet, it also insists on Boccaccio's own place in the select company of Petrarch and the other poets named here: Sennuccio del Bene, Cino da Pistoia, and Dante Alighieri. He deems himself as worthy of inclusion on the basis of a communal friendship, his life as a poet, and a lyric enterprise spanning four decades. The *rime,* despite Boccaccio's own seeming disregard for them and their constant marginalization by critics over the centuries, are a testament to his inclusion among that illustrious company of poets.

Akash Kumar
University of California, Berkeley

13 See Vecchi Galli, *Padri: Petrarca e Boccaccio nella poesia del Trecento* (Rome: Antenore, 2012), 77.

Rime

1

Le parole söave e 'l dolce riso,
la treccia d'oro, che 'l cor m'ha legato
e messo nelle man' che m'hanno ucciso
già mille volte e 'n vita ritornato
di nuovo, m'hanno sì 'l petto infiammato
che tutto il mio desire al vago viso
rivolto s'è; ed altro non m'è grato
che di vederlo e di mirarlo fiso.

In quel mi par veder quant'allegrezza
che fa beati gli occhi de' mortali
che si fan degni d'eterna salute;
in quel risplende chiara la bellezza
che 'l ciel adorna e che n'impenna l'ali
a l'alto vol con penne di virtute.

2

Spesso m'avvien ch'essendom'io raccolto
co' miei pensier', partito dalla gente,
senza donde veder, nella mia mente
se n' vien colei nel cui celeste volto
la mia salute sta, e che, disciolto,
ne' legami d'Amor söavemente
con gli occhi sua mi pose, e lietamente
a sé tir'ogni spirto altrove vòlto.

Poi ragionand'a llor fa riguardare
la sua virtù, la bellezza e 'l valore,
d'i quai più ch'altra l'ha dotata Dio:
dond'un piacer mi nasce, el qual mi pare
che rechi seco ciò che puote Amore
e sol accenda a ben far il disio.

1

Her choice of gentle words and her sweet smile,
her golden tresses, which have bound my heart
and placed it in her hands that caused my death
a thousand times ere now and brought me back
to life again, have so inflamed my heart
that my desire has all reverted to
her lovely face; and nothing pleases me
except to look and firmly gaze on it.

I seem to see in it a happiness
that makes the eyes of mortals blessed
who then grow worthy of eternal bliss;
in it I see her beauty shining bright,
adorning heaven and empowering
our wings to fly above on virtue's quills.

2

It often happens when I'm lost in thought
and find myself apart from company,
that in my mind, without my knowing from where,
there comes the one in whose celestial face
dwells my salvation, which, since I am free,
enwraps me gently in the bonds of Love
by means of her fair eyes, and joyfully
pulls towards itself all spirits turned elsewhere.

Then speaking to them it makes them regard
her virtue, beauty, and her worthiness,
which more than any woman God gave her:
from this a pleasure comes to me, which seems
to bring with it what Love's empowered to do
and only spurs desire to do what's good.

3

Com'io vi veggo, bella donna e cara,
così mi sento per gli occhi passare
una söavità la qual mi pare
che del cor cacci ogni passione amara
e pongavi un desio, el qual rischiara
ogni pensier turbato e che stimare
mi fa voi di bellezza trapassare
al mond'ogn'altra: sola, unica, o cara!

E quiv'i' lodo la fortuna mia
ed Amor, che a voi mi fé subbietto
come m'apparve la vostra figura.
Né più oltre la mia mente desia
che di poter, con onestà, diletto
prestar a così bella crëatura.

4

Con quanta affezïon io vi rimiri
a voi non posson celar gli occhi miei,
li quai de' vostri, sì com'io vorrei,
credon, quei riguardando, trar sospiri
che portin pace a ben mille martirî
che nascon del desio ch'io non potei
quel dì frenar – ch'è arbitrio delli dei –
d'entrar per voi negli amorosi giri.

E se quei che nel mio petto portaro
con amore speranza non mi sono
benigni, da cui dunque aspetto pace?
Io non dimando al vostro onor contraro,
ma mi facciate d'un sospiro dono,
il qual mitighi il foco che mi sface.

3

While I am gazing on you, beautiful
dear lady, I feel passing through my eyes
a sweetness that appears to me to chase
away all bitter passions from my heart
and place there a desire that mollifies
my troubled thoughts and makes me rank
your beauty as surpassing that of all
who live on earth: O sole, unique, dear one!

And I praise here my good fortune and Love,
which made me subject to your dominance
when you came into view before my eyes.
My mind has no desire for anything
except to have the power, quite honestly,
to give delight to one so beautiful.

4

With how much tenderness I gaze on you
my eyes cannot conceal from you at all,
and they believe that they draw sighs from yours,
while looking at them, as I'd like to think,
which bring peace to at least a thousand wounds
that come from the desire which I could not
hold back that day – the gods decide – to pass
because of you into the dance of love.

And so if they who brought into my heart
with love some hope are not benevolent,
from whom may I then seek to purchase peace?
I ask for nothing that would undermine
your honour, but impart to me a sigh,
to mitigate the fire that ruins me.

5

Sì dolcemente a' sua lacci m'adesca
Amor, con gli occhi vaghi di costei,
che, quanto più m'allontano da lei,
più vi tira 'l desio e più l'invesca:
per ch'io non veggio come mai me n'èsca,
e certo rïuscirne non vorrei,
tanto contenta tutti e desir' miei
i suoi costumi e l'onestà donnesca.

Chi vuol si doglia e piangasi d'Amore,
ch'io me ne lodo per insino ad ora,
se più non m'arde il caro signor mio;
e benedico quel vago splendore
che 'l cor sì dolcemente m'innamora,
allumandomi sì, ch'io son più ch'io.

6

Biasiman molti spiacevoli Amore
e dicon lui accidente noioso,
pien di spavento, cupido e ritroso,
e di sospir' cortese donatore.
Né vede di costoro il cieco errore
come proceda il suo valor nascoso
nell'uom prudent'e giusto ed animoso
a, per bene operar, volere onore.

Come costui nell'anima gentile
pronto si pon per valoroso obbietto,
così la rende cortese e umìle.
Ornarsi di costumi è 'l suo diletto;
fugge come nimico, ogn'atto vile:
chi dunque dè cessar starli subbietto?

5

So sweetly Love entraps me in his snares
with her alluring eyes that the further
I move away from her the more he spurs
desire for them, ensnaring it yet more;
and so I don't see how I could escape
from her, and surely that I would not want,
so greatly do her noble virtuousness
and conduct satisfy all my desires.

Let those who wish feel pain and weep for Love,
for up to now I have but praise for him,
if my dear master doesn't burn me more;
and I extol the lovely radiance
that enamours my heart so sweetly that,
enlightening me so much, I'm more than I.

6

Now many who are crude disparage Love
and claim it is a painful accident
that rouses fear and lust, and bashfulness,
and is a lavish donor of deep sighs.
Their blind mistake means they don't understand
just how its hidden power operates
in one who's wise and just and is inspired
to seek esteem in order to do good.

Just as it renders in the noble mind
a keenness to achieve a worthy end,
so does it make one humble and refined.
To show its etiquette is its delight;
it flees what's worthless as its enemy:
who then should cease to be its devotee?

7

Questo amoroso fuoco è sì soave
che tuttora ardo, e parmi crescer vita;
ma vedo ben che, se 'l ciel non m'aita,
rotta è fra duro scoglio la mia nave.
Tal mi tien chiuso sotto a mille chiave
che, con sua faccia angelica e polita,
or pena eterna or dolcezza infinita
mi mostra; or m'assicura, or mi spave.

Così, del mio fin dubio ardendo, spero
nel fuoco rinovar come fenice:
e questo d'ogni doglia è medicina.
Né posso, mio giudicio, dir con vero
che per cosa terrena esser felice
io cerchi, ma d'effigie alta e divina.

8

Quello spirto vezzoso che nel core
mi misero i begli occhi di costei
parla sovente con meco di lei
leggiadramente, e simile d'Amore.
E poi del suo animoso fervore
una speranza crea ne' pensier' miei
che sì lieto mi fa, ch'io mi potrei
bëato dir s'ella stesse molt'ore.

Ma un tremor, da non so che paura
nato, lo scaccia e rompe in mezzo il porto,
ch'aver preso credea, di mia salute;
e veggio aperto ch'alcun ben non dura
lunga stagione in questo viver corto,
quantunque possa natural virtute.

7

This fire of love's so pleasant that I burn
incessantly, and yet it nurtures life;
but I can see if heaven brings no help
my ship will break apart upon the rocks.
She keeps me locked up with so many keys
that with her brilliant and angelic face,
now ceaseless pain, now sweetness infinite
she shows me; now she soothes, now she alarms.

So, burning from my piercing doubt, I hope
to come back like the phoenix from the fire:
and this is medicine for all my pain.
I cannot, in my judgment, truly say
that I'm in search of earthly happiness,
but of the image of the heavenly.

8

The spirit that is full of graciousness
which her fair eyes have put into my heart
speaks frequently and tenderly to me
of her, and so too does it speak of Love.
And then from its intense vitality
it generates a hope within my thoughts
that makes me feel so happy I could say
I'm blessed if only it would last a while.

A tremor, then, arising from some fear,
repulses it and sinks it out at sea,
when I thought I had safely come to shore;
and I can clearly see that no good lasts
for any length of time in this short life,
despite the power that natural virtue has.

9

Misero me! ch'io non oso mirare
gli occhi ne' quali stava la mia pace:
però che, come il ghiaccio si disface
al sol, così mi sento il cor disfare
per soverchio disio nel riguardare;
e, s'altro miro, tanto mi dispiace
ch'un gel noioso vienmi, il qual mi fàce
di morte spesse volte dubitare.

Tra questi estrem'i' sto, né so che farmi:
o arder tutto, lor mirando fiso,
o di freddo morire, altro guardando.
L'un mi duol men, ma troppo grave parmi
da cui salute spero esser ucciso,
e più duro mi par morir guardando!

10

Pallido, vinto e tutto transmutato
dallo stato primier quando mi vede
la nemica d'amore e di mercede
nelle cui reti son preso e legato,
quasi di ciò che io ho già contato
del suo valor, prendendo intera fede,
lieta più preme il cor che la possede,
indi sperando nome più pregiato.

Ond'io stimo che sia da mutar verso,
pur ch'Amor me l' consenta, e biasimare
ciò che io scioccamente già lodai.
Forse diverrà bianco il color perso,
e per lo non ben dir potrò impetrare,
per avventura, fine alli mia guai.

9

Unhappy me! for I don't dare to look
upon the eyes in which my peace once dwelled:
thus, just as ice melts in the sun, I feel
my heart dissolve because of my desire
in looking at her so excessively;
and if I look away, I am dismayed
so much a painful chill comes over me,
which often brings to me the fear of death.

I'm caught between extremes, and don't know what
to do: burn up by looking straight at them,
or freeze to death by looking somewhere else.
The first hurts less, but it seems too severe
to die by her in whom I look for bliss,
yet harder to die looking somewhere else!

10

When the enemy of love and mercy
in whose nets I am seized and wholly bound
observes me pale, defeated, utterly
transfigured from my former state of being,
considering that it is true what I
said earlier about her worthiness,
my heart which she possesses she torments
more gladly, hoping to gain greater fame.

So I conclude that I must change my tack,
as long as Love approves, and place the fault
on what I foolishly have praised before.
Perhaps the color perse will turn to white,
and for the fault that I have made, I can,
perhaps, plead for an end to all my woe.

11

Quando poss'io sperar che mai conforme
divegna questa donna a' desir' miei?
ch'ancor con prieghi impetrar non potei
dal Sonno, mostrator di mille forme,
ch'in sogn'almen dov'ella lascia l'orme
mi dimonstrasse: e contento sarei,
poi ch'io non posso più riveder lei,
che crudel cerca, lasso!, in terra porme.

Allora certo, quando torneranno
li fiumi a' monti, e i lupi l'agnelle
dagli ovil', temorosi, fuggiranno.
Dunque uccidimi, Amore, acciò che quelle
luci, che fûr principio del mio danno,
del morir mio ridendo, sien più belle!

12

Son certi augei sì vaghi della luce
ch'avendogli la notte già riposti
nel lor albergo e dentro a sé nascosti,
dèsti da picciol suono, ove traluce
quantunque picciol lume, gli conduce
il desio d'esso; al qual seguir disposti,
dove diletto cercan, ne' sopposti
lacci sottentron drieto al falso duce.

Lasso!, così sovent'e' m'addiviene:
ché, dove io sento dal voler chiamarmi
drieto a' begli occhi e falsi di costei,
presto vi corro: e da nuove catene
legar mi veggio, onde di scaprestarmi,
stolto, speravo, per rimirar lei.

11

When can I hope my lady will one day
become agreeable to my desires?
For I've not yet been able to obtain
by prayer from Sleep, the fabricator of
a thousand forms, at least some sign of where
she is; and I would be content, since I
no longer can see her again, who tries,
alas!, to cast me cruelly to the ground.

So certainly, when streams flow backward to
the hills, and when the wolves, beset by fear,
flee from the lambkins huddled in their pen.
So kill me, Love, in order that those lights,
which were the origin of all my woe,
shine lovelier, from laughing at my death!

12

Some birds are so attracted to the light
that after night's already sheltered them
within their nests and kept them hidden in
the dark, awakened by some little sound,
where light, however faint, appears, desire
draws them to it; disposed to follow it,
in seeking out delight, they enter traps
that are unseen, led there by treachery.

Alas!, this often happens too with me:
for when I feel myself called by desire,
drawn by her lovely and deceptive eyes,
I quickly come, and find I'm in new chains,
whereas I'd hoped to find myself set free,
being but a fool, to see her once again.

13

Le lagrime e i sospiri e il non sperare
a quelle fine m'han sì sbigottito,
ch'io me ne vo per via com'uom smarrito:
non so che dire e molto men che fare.
E quand'avvien che talor ragionare
oda di me – ché n'ho tal volta udito –,
del pallido color e del partito
vigore e del dolor che di fuor pare,

una pietà di me stesso mi viene
sì grande, ch'io desio di dir piangendo
chi sia cagion di tanto mio martiro.
Ma poi, temendo non aggiugner pene
alle mia noie, tanto mi difendo
ch'io passo in compagnia d'alcun sospiro.

14

S'e' mi bastasse allo scriver l'ingegno
la mirabil bellezza e 'l gran valore
di quella donna, a cui diede il mio core
Amor, della mia fede eterno pegno,
ed ancora l'angoscia ch'io sostegno
o per lo suo o per lo mio errore,
veggendo me della sua grazia fore
esser sospinto da crudele sdegno,

io mostrerrei assai chiaro ed aperto
che 'l pianger mio e 'l mio esser ismorto
maraviglia non sia, ma ch'io sia vivo.
Ma poi non posso, ciaschedun sia certo
ch'egli è assai maggiore il duol ch'io porto
che 'l mio viso non monstra e ch'io non scrivo.

13

My tears and sighs and not expecting them
to cease have so dumbfounded me that I
now go along my way like one who's lost:
I don't know what to say, less what to do.
And when it happens that I sometimes hear
I'm talked about – for so I've heard at times –
regarding my pale colour and my loss
of strength and pain that shows upon my face,

a pity for myself comes over me
so great that, weeping, I desire to tell
who is the cause of my deep suffering.
But fearing, then, that this will add more pain
to my distress, so much do I hold back
that I pass time together with a sigh.

14

Had I sufficient talent to describe
that lady's wondrous beauty and great worth,
the one to whom Love gave my heart, the pledge
of my eternal faith, and to describe
as well the agony that I endure
because of error on her part or mine,
and seeing how I'm driven out of her
good graces by implacable disdain,

I'd show with clarity and openness
that my lamenting and my pallidness
are no surprise, but that I still live is.
But since I can't, let everyone know well
that greater is by far the pain I bear
than what my face reveals and what I write.

15

Così ben fusse inteso il mio parlare
come l'intende i caldi sospir' mei:
ché, bench'io viva in pianti acerbi e rei,
un gioco mi parrebbe a lacrimare.
Ma, s'io potesse alquanto dichiarare
l'animo mio doglioso a chi vorrei,
son certo che poche ore viverei
fra tante angosce e tante pene amare:

ïo farei quei begli occhi pietosi,
che, quando lacrimando a lor m'inchino,
non mi sarebbon fieri e disdegnosi.
Ond'io prego il mio fato e il mio destino
che porgan qualche luce a' tenebrosi
spirti c'hanno a far sì alto camino.

16

Benché si fosse, per la tuo partita,
l'alta speranza, la qual io prendea
de' tuo vaghi occhi, qualor gli vedea,
giovine bella, quasi che fuggita,
pur sostenea la deboletta vita
un söave pensier, che mi dicea,
quando di ciò co·meco mi dolea:
"Tosto sarà omai la suo reddita!".

Ma ciò mai non avene, e me partire
or convien contra grado, né speranza
di mai vederti mi rimane alcuna:
onde morrommi, caro mio disire,
e piangerò, il tempo che mi avanza,
lontano a te, la mie crudel fortuna.

15

If only what I say were understood
the way my ardent sighings understand:
for though I live in bitter, evil pain,
to weep would seem to be a kind of joy.
But if I could at least say that my mind
is racked with pain to the one whom I'd wish,
I'm sure I'd have to live but little time
with such great anguish and such bitter pain:

I'd make those lovely eyes be merciful,
which, when I bow before them crying tears,
would not be haughty and contemptuous.
So I beseech my fate and destiny
to cast some light upon my gloomy spirits
that have to travel on so hard a path.

16

Although, because you have departed now,
my highest hope, which I would gather from
your lovely eyes whenever I'd see them,
my fair young girl, has almost fled away,
yet still a tender thought would bring care to
my fragile life, which used to say to me,
whenever I was suffering from it:
"It won't be long now till she has returned!"

But that's not happened yet, and I must now
depart against my will, because no hope
remains for me to see you once again.
So I will die, my dearest fond desire,
and I will weep, throughout the rest of life,
my cruel misfortune, being far from you.

17

Poscia che gli occhi mia la vaga vista
hanno perduta, il cui lieto splendore
ciaschedun mio desir caldo d'amore
facea contento in questa valle trista,
dove più noia chi più vive acquista,
non curo omai se del dolente core,

alma, te n' vai, perciò che 'l mio dolore
non regolerà mai discreto artista.
Anzi te n' va', ch'io, che solea cantare,
non vo' pascer l'invidia di coloro
a' quai doler solea la mia letizia.
Vatten adunque omai: non aspettare
d'esser cacciata; ed altrove ristoro
prendi, se puoi, di questa mia trestizia.

18

Deh, quanto è greve la mïe sventura
e mobile più ch'altro il viver mio!
Io piango spesso con tanto disio
quant'alcun rida: e, mentre il pianto dura,
vien nella mente mia quella figura
che più ch'altro mi piace: sallo Iddio.
Quivi col lieto aspetto vago e pio
conforta 'l core e l'alma rassicura

dicendo cose ch'ogni spiritello
smarrito surge lieto e pien d'amore,
e me fan più ch'alcun altro contento.
Di quinci nasce chi dal viso bello
mi mostra esser lontano: onde 'l dolore
torna più fier che prima per un cento.

17

Ever since my eyes have lost the sight
that is so fair, whose joyful radiance
would bring delight to all my passionate
desire in this vale of unhappiness,
where longer life means greater tedium,
I now no longer care that you should leave
my wounded heart, dear soul, because my pain
can't ever be expressed by rules of art.

Just go away, for I, who used to sing,
don't want to feed upon the jealousy
of those whom my delight was cause for pain.
And so, now, go away: and do not wait
to be thrown out; and elsewhere find yourself
relief, if you are able, from my gloom.

18

Alas, how sad is my adversity
and most of all how mutable my life!
I often weep with deep desire as much
as some do when they laugh: and, while my cries
persist, there comes into my mind the image
that pleases most of all: and this God knows.
Here with her happy, lovely, holy face
she calms my heart and reassures my soul

by speaking words that make all my confused
small spirits waken glad and full of love,
and they content me more than anything.
From this a thought arises showing me
that I am far from her fair face: so pain
more than a hundred times as fierce returns.

19

O miseri occhi miei più ch'altra cosa,
piangete omai, piangete, e non restate!
Voi di colei le luci dispietate
menasti pria nell'anima angosciosa,
ch'ora disprezza; voi nell'amorosa
pregion legaste la mia libertate;
voi col mirarla più raccendevate
il cor dolente, ch'or non truova posa.

Dunque piangete, e la nemica vista
di voi spingete col pianger più forte,
sì ch'altro amor non possa più tradirvi.
Questo desia e vuol l'anima trista,
perciò che cose grave più che morte
l'ordisti già incontro nel seguirvi.

20

Chi nel suo pianger dice che ventura
avversa gli è al suo maggior disio;
e chi l'appone sciocamente a Dio;
e chi accusa Amore, e chi la dura
condizïon della donna che, pura,
forse non sente l'appetito rio;
e chi del cielo fa ramarichio,
non conoscendo sé, di sua sciagura.

Ma io, dolente, solo agli occhi miei
ogni mia doglia appongo, che fûr porte
all'amorosa *fiamma* che mi sface.
Se stati fosser chiusi, ancor potrei,
signor di me, contrastar alla Morte,
la qual or chiamo per mia dolce pace.

19

O my unhappy eyes more than all else,
go on and weep, go weep, and do not stop!
You brought those unforgiving eyes of her
initially into my anguished soul,
which she now scorns; you took my liberty
and bound it in the prison house of love;
by looking at her you've set fire again
to my sad heart, which now can find no rest.

So, weep, and chase away the hostile sight
you see with weeping that is stronger still,
to keep some other love from cheating you.
My saddened soul desires and wishes this,
since you've already schemed to do to her
things worse than death while she was watching you.

20

Some claim, distraught, it's fortune that's averse
to what they most of all desire to have;
and others foolishly say God's the cause;
and others still blame Love, and others yet
the callous nature of the woman who,
being chaste, perhaps does not feel base desire;
and some place blame for their adversity
upon the stars, and not upon themselves.

But I, forlorn, place all my suffering
upon my eyes alone, the entry point
used by the *flame* of love that ruins me.
Had they been closed, I might have had a chance,
as master of myself, to fight off Death,
which I now call upon to bring sweet peace.

21

Cader postù in que' legami, Amore,
ne' quai tu n'hai già molti aviluppati;
rotte ti sien le braccia, ed ispuntati
gli artigli, e l'ali spennate, e 'l vigore
tolto, e la deïtà tua sia 'n orrore
a quei che nasceran e che son nati,
e sianti l'arco e gli strali spezzati,
e il tuo nome sia sempre Dolore!

Bugiardo, traditore e disleale,
frodolente, assassin, ladro, scherano,
crudel tiranno, spergiuro, omicida!
ché, dopo il mio lungo servire invano,
mi proponesti tal, ch'assai men vale:
caggia dal ciel saetta che t'occida!

22

Se io potessi creder ch'in cinqu'anni,
che gli è che vostro fui, tanto caluto
di me vi fosse che aver saputo
il nome mio voleste de' mia danni
per ristorato avermi, de' mia affanni
potrei forse sperare ancora aiuto;
né mi parrebbe il tempo aver perduto
a condolermi de' mia stessi inganni.

Ma poich'egli è così, come sperare
posso merzé? come fin all'ardore,
che, quanto meno spero, è più cocente?
So si dovria cotal amor lasciare;
ma, non potendo, moro di dolore,
cagion essendo voi del fin dolente.

21

May you be captured, Love, and tied in bonds
in which you have already many bound;
your arms be broken, and your talons shorn,
your wings defeathered, and your power stripped,
may your divinity seem horrifying
to those who will be born and those alive,
and may your bow and arrows be destroyed,
and your name always be allied with Pain!

You are a liar, traitor, and untrue,
assassin, swindler, thief, and ruffian,
a ruthless tyrant, killer, perjurer!
For, after serving you in vain for years,
you favoured one who is of much less worth:
may lightning from the sky now strike you dead!

22

If I believed that during those five years,
the time when I was yours, you cared for me
so much that when you heard my name you wished
to compensate me for the injuries
that you imposed on me, perhaps I might
still harbour hope for help for all my grief;
nor would it seem that I have wasted time
in feeling pain for having been deceived.

But since that's how it is, how can I hope
for mercy? or an end to my desire,
which burns me more the less I hope for it?
I know I should leave such a love as this;
but not being able to, I die of pain,
and you're the reason for my painful end.

23

"O iniquo uomo, o servo disleale,
di che ti duol? di che vai lagrimando?
di che Amor e me vai biasimando
quasi cagion del tuo noioso male?
Qual arco apers'io mai, o quale strale
ti säettai? quai prieghi, o dove, o quando
ti fûr fatti per me, che, me amando,
mi dessi il cor, di cui sì or ti cale?

Pregastù me, e scongiurasti Amore
ch'io t'avessi per mio: qual dunque inganno,
qual crudeltà t'è fatta? del mio onore
mi cal più troppo che del tuo affanno".
Così Fiammetta par talor nel core
mi dica: ond'io mi doglio ed hommi il danno.

24

Non deve alcuno, per pena soffrire,
quanto che 'l tempo paia longo o sia,
gittar del tutto la speranza via
o stoltamente cercar di morire:
ché un'ora sola può sopravenire,
la qual discaccia onne fortuna ria
e sì consola altrui che l'omo oblia
danno e dolor e fatica e martìre.

Ed io el so, el qual già longamente
chiesi mercé con doloroso pianto
agli occhi bei, che già fûr dispiatati;
e non sperando ciò, subitamente
Amor i mie suspir' rivolse in canto,
e sento la letizia d'i beati.

23

"O wicked man, O servant most disloyal,
what troubles you? What makes you go on crying?
Why do you go on blaming me and Love
for being the cause of your heart-rending grief?
What bow have I drawn, ever, what shaft have
I shot at you? What pleas, say when, tell where,
did I make you, so, loving me, you would
give me your heart, which now concerns you so?

You prayed to me, and you begged Love for me
to have you as my own: so, what deceit,
what cruelty was done to you? I hold
my honour more important than your grief."
So Fiammetta seems to say at times
inside my heart, which pains and injures me.

24

No one, for being in a state of pain,
however long the time may seem or be,
should throw away all hope entirely
or foolishly attempt to end one's life.
For just a single hour may occur
that makes all adverse fortune disappear
and brings relief so that one will forget
the harm and pain and toil and sacrifice.

And I know well that I already have
at length sought mercy with my painful cries
before your lovely eyes, which once were cruel;
and then against all hope, Love suddenly
turned all my sighing into melody,
and now I feel the bliss of those in heaven.

25

Fuggano i sospir' miei, fuggasi il pianto,
fugga l'angoscia e fuggasi el disio
che aùto ho di morir! Vada in oblio
ciò che contra ad Amor già pensai tanto!
Torni la festa, torni 'l riso e 'l canto!
Torni gli onor' devuti al signor mio,
li meriti del qual han fatto ch'io
aggia la grazia bramata cotanto!

Lo sdegno, el qual a torto me negava
el vago sguardo degli occhi lucenti
coi qual' Amor mi prese, è tolto via;
e quel saluto ch'io più desïava
con umil voce e con atti piacenti
pur testé mi rendé la donna mia.

26

Amor, se questa donna non s'infinge,
la mia speranza al suo termine viene,
perciò che, ogni volta ch'egli avviene
che tu o forza di destin mi spinge
dov'ella sia, così 'l viso dipinge
di pallidezza sùbita e non tiene
le luci ferme, ma di desio piene,
ora ver' me l'allarga ed or le stringe;

e sì vinta si mostra dai sospiri
che 'n vista par che sol prieghi per pace,
contenta ch'ïo in tale atto la miri.
Io che farò, che nella tua fornace
ardo, premuto da mille desiri?
non arderò poi vegg'io ch'e' le piace?

25

My sighs, be gone with you, my cries, be gone,
my suffering, be gone, and my desire
that I myself must die, be gone! Be now
forgotten what I once held against Love!
Let joy return, let mirth and song return!
Let honours owed my master Love return,
the worthiness allowing me to have
the graciousness that I have so desired!

Her scorn, which wrongfully denied to me
the lovely glance of her resplendent eyes,
by which Love seized me, has been swept away;
and, too, the greeting that I most of all
desired with humble voice and pleasing deeds
my lady has just now conferred on me.

26

Love, if this lady is not insincere,
my hope will finally have come near its goal,
so every time that it should come to pass
that you or force of destiny leads me
to where she is, she so bedecks her face
with pallidness and cannot make her eyes
stay firm, but laden with desire, towards me
she opens and she closes them by turns;

and she displays herself so seized by sighs
her face suggests she only prays for peace,
content for me to see her in that pose.
What should I do, since I am being burned
inside your kiln and crushed by fierce desire?
Should I not burn, then, seeing it pleases her?

27

Se quel serpente che guarda il tesoro
del qual m'ha fatto Amor tanto bramoso
ponesse pur un poco el capo gióso,
io crederrei con un sottil lavoro
trovar al pianto mio alcun ristoro;
né in ciò sarebbe il mio cor temoroso,
come che già, in punto assai dubbioso,
già mi negasse il promess'adiutoro.

Ma pria Mercurio chiuderà que' d'Argo
cantando di Siringa che 'n que' due
io possa metter sonno col mio verso;
e prima nelle lagrime ch'io spargo
morendo adempierò le voglie tue,
crudel Amor, ver' me fiero e perverso!

28

Il folgór de' begli occhi, el qual m'avampa
il cor qualor io gli riguardo fiso,
m'è tanto nella mente, ov'io l'ho miso
spesso, segnato con eterna stampa,
ch'invan, caro signore, ogn'altra vampa
ver' me saetti del tuo paradiso:
questo m'allegra, questo m'ha conquiso,
questo m'uccide, questo ancor mi scampa.

Dunque, ti prego, al tuo arco perdona,
e bastiti per una avermi preso:
ch'assai è gran legame questo e forte.
E mentre 'l tuo valor la sua persona
farà più bella, sì com'è testeso,
mai non mi scioglierà se non la Morte.

27

If the serpent that protects my treasure
for which Love made me hunger with desire
let down its guard for just a little while,
I think by working skillfully I'd find
some consolation for my anguished tears;
my heart would not be fearful doing this,
since once before, at a most crucial point,
it had already denied promised help.

But Mercury will first close Argos's eyes
by singing of Syrinx before I can
put his two eyes to sleep with my own song;
and first of all, with tears that I will shed
I shall fulfill your wishes as I die,
cruel Love, depraved and arrogant towards me.

28

The splendour of your eyes, which sets my heart
on fire when I gaze steadily on them,
is so imprinted in my mind, where I
have often placed it, etched eternally,
that every other flame you shoot towards me
from paradise, dear sir, is shot in vain:
one makes me happy, one has conquered me,
another kills me, that one goes astray.

Therefore, I beg you put aside your bow,
let it suffice that you struck me with one:
for this one greatly holds me fast and tight.
As long as your abundant might makes her
more beautiful, as it does presently,
it will not ever let me go till Death.

29

Se quella *fiamma* che nel cor m'accese
ed or mi sface in doloroso pianto
fosse ver' me pietosa pur alquanto
e del monstrarsi un poco più cortese,
ancora spererei trovar difese
alla mia vita, che m'è in odio tanto,
e ' sospir' grevi rivolger in canto
e poter perdonar le fatte offese.

Ma perché, come Febo fuggì Dane,
così costei d'ogni parte mi fugge
e niega agli occhi miei il suo bel lume,
troppo invescata in l'amorose pane
la vita mia cognosco che si strugge
e 'l cor diventa di lagrime fiume.

30

Quando s'accese quella prima *fiamma*
dentro da me che 'l cor mi munge ed arde,
io solia dir talor: "Questa non arde
come suol arder ciascun'altra fiamma;
anzi conforta, sospigne ed infiamma
a valor seguitar chiunque ella arde:
per ch'esser dè contento, in cui ella arde,
di più fin divenir in cotal fiamma".

Ma il cor, già carbon fatto in questo foco,
senza pace sperar, in tristo pianto,
ha mutata sentenzia e chiede morte.
E non trovando lei in cotal foco,
ora rovente ed or bagnato in pianto,
si sta in vita assai peggior che morte.

29

If that *flame* which has set my heart afire
and now destroys me with grief-stricken tears
were merciful towards me for just a while
and showed itself somewhat more generous,
I would still hope to find protection for
my life, which is so odious to me,
and turn my grievous sighing into song
and find the strength to pardon my offenses.

But since, as Daphne turned and fled from Phoebus,
she, too, flees everywhere away from me
denying my eyes the sight of her fair light,
I know my life's become far too beset
by love's deceits, consuming it with pain,
and so my heart becomes engulfed with tears.

30

When that *flame* first began to blaze in me
which drains my heart of strength and makes it burn,
I used to say at times: "This does not burn
as every other flame is wont to burn;
it, rather, comforts, urges, and inflames
to follow virtue whomever it burns:
because he must be pleased, the one it burns,
to become more refined in such a flame."

But my heart, turned to ashes by this fire
already, with no hope of peace, in tears
of woe, has changed its view and now seeks death.
And so not finding it in such a fire,
now scorching hot, now dripping wet with tears,
it has a life that is much worse than death.

31

Quella splendida *fiamma* il cui fulgore
m'aperse prima l'amorosa via
m'incende sì, qualor l'anima mia
vola colà dove la chiama Amore,
che 'l troppo lume el debile valore
degli occhi abbaglia sì, che la si svia
dal debito sentier, e dove sia
né sa, né vede, d'ogni ragion fuore.

E mentre così erra tremebonda,
fa di me rider chi allor mi vede,
e tal fïata alcun muove a pietate.
Laond'e' segue che 'l desio, ch'abbonda,
discuovre ciò che nasconder si crede
la disvïata fuor di libertate.

32

Il gran disio che l'amorosa *fiamma*
nel cuor m'accese nei miei miglior' anni,
e tiene ancor crescendo ciascun giorno
e terrà forse insino a l'ultim'ora,

tolto ha da me ciascun altro desire:
e com li piace mi si fa seguire.
....

31

That dazzling *flame* whose radiance first made
the path of love accessible to me,
inflames me so, whenever my soul flies
where Love has summoned it, that too much light
subdues the feeble power of my eyes
and forces it to leave the proper path,
and where it is it does not know or see,
because it lacks the power to think and will.

And while it wanders trembling constantly,
whoever sees me then begins to laugh,
and it makes some feel pity now and then.
And so it follows that my deep desire,
so full, reveals that which the wayward soul,
deprived of liberty, attempts to hide.

32

The great desire that the *flame* of love
awakened in my heart in my best years,
and still keeps growing stronger every day
and will, perhaps, right up to my last hour,

has taken from me every other desire:
and as it wants I'm forced to follow it.
....

33

Quell'amorosa luce il cui splendore
per li miei occhi mise le faville
che, dentr'al cor andando a mille a mille,
di lei la forma e la luce d'Amore,
– questa per donna e colui per signore –
lasciaronvi non posson le pupille
soffrir talor per l'acute postille
ch'accese vengon più del suo valore.

Onde, contra mia voglia, s'io non voglio
lei riguardando perder di vederla,
in altra part'e' mi convien voltare.
O grieve caso ond'io forte mi doglio:
colei cui cerco di veder poterla
sempre, non posso poi lei riguardare!

34

Se bionde trecce, chioma crespa e d'oro,
occhi ridenti, splendidi e söavi,
atti piacevoli e costumi gravi,
sentito motteggiare, onesto e soro
parlar in donna, com'in suo tesoro,
pose natura mai, o finser savi:
tutt'è 'n costei, Amor, in cui le chiavi
delle mia pene desti e del ristoro.

Dunque, se io sovente ne sospiro,
non mi riprenda chi la mia speranza
non vede posta in premio del martiro.
Questa li mia pensier' urge e avanza
con gli occhi sua a sì alto desiro
che nulla più sentir have 'n possanza.

33

That loving light whose splendour introduced
into my eyes the sparks that, entering
my heart so many thousands at a time,
implanted there a portrait and Love's light,
– this one of her and that one of the lord –
my pupils are unable to endure
at times because of the bright images
that shine more strongly than the light's own power.

And so, against my will, if I don't want
to lose my sight of her by watching her,
I need to turn around and look away.
Oh, what a blow that brings such grievous pain:
the one whom I am always trying to see
is she whom I'm not able to regard!

34

If locks of curly golden hair, blonde braids,
resplendent, smiling eyes, so delicate,
delightful gestures, noble character,
tactful speech, an honest gentle way
in speaking womanly, it being her treasure,
did nature ever make or poets sing,
they're found in her, sir Love, to whom you gave
the keys of my distress and comforting.

So, if this often causes me to sigh,
let no one censure me who cannot see
that my reward for hoping is fulfilled.
She quickens and encourages my thoughts
with her eyes filled with such intense desire
no other sentiment is possible.

35

Mai non potei, per mirar molto fiso
i rossi labri e gli occhi vaghi e belli,
il viso tutto e gli aureï capelli
di questa che m'è in Terra un paradiso,
nell'intelletto comprender preciso
qual più mirabil si fosse di quelli:
come ch'io stimo di preporre ad elli
l'angelico, leggiadro e dolce riso;

nel qual, quando scintillan quelle stelle
che la luce del ciel fanno minore,
par s'apra il cielo e rida il mondo tutto.
Ond'io, che tutto 'l cor ho dritto a quelle,
esser mi tengo molto di megliore
sentend'in Terra sì celeste frutto.

36

Qualor mi mena Amor dov'io vi veggia
– ch'assai di rado avvien, sì cara siete –,
l'anima, piena d'amorosa sete,
come la luce vede che lampeggia
da' bei vostri occhi, nel pensier vaneggia:
quello sperando ch'ancor non volete
– ciò è saziarsi, come voi vedete,
di mirarvi –, focosa vi vagheggia.

E com'è stolto il mio vago pensiero!
Là ond'io credo refrigerio avere,
accese fiamme attingo a mill'a mille;
ma come cuocan non sento, nel vero,
mentre egli avvien ch'io vi possa vedere;
ma poi, partito, m'ardon le faville.

35

I never could, however much I gazed
intently on the ruby lips, the eyes
so fair, the entire face and golden hair
of this one who's my paradise on Earth,
grasp with a clarity of intellect
which of these features was most wonderful;
and yet I deem as preferable to them
her elegant, angelic and sweet smile,

in which, whenever those stars scintillate
that make the light up in the sky less bright,
the sky grows visible and the world laughs.
So I, who have turned all my heart towards them,
consider myself to be much improved
in seeing such celestial fruit on Earth.

36

Whenever Love leads me where I see you
– which happens rarely, since you are so prized –
my soul, completely full of thirst for love,
as soon as it sees light that flashes forth
from your attractive eyes, becomes confused:
in hope of having what you do not wish
– which, as you see, is to be satisfied
with seeing you – it fiercely yearns for you.

How foolish now is this sweet thought of mine!
Where I think I might purchase some relief,
I feel a hundred thousand scorching flames;
but truly I don't feel how hot they are
as long as I am able to see you;
but after I have left, I'm burned by sparks.

37

Candide perle orïentali e nuove
sotto vivi rubin' chiari e vermigli,
da' quali un riso angelico si muove
che sfavillar sotto due neri cigli
sovente insieme fa Vener e Giove,
e con vermiglie rose i bianchi gigli
misti fa il suo colore in ogni dove,
senza che arte alcuna s'assottigli:

i capei d'oro e crespi un lume fanno
sovra la lieta fronte, entr'alla quale
Amore abbaglia della maraviglia;
e l'altre parti tutte si confanno
alle predette, in proporzion eguale,
di costei ch'i ver' angioli simiglia.

38

Quel dolce canto col qual già Orfeo
Cerbero vinse e il nocchier d'Acheronte,
o quel con ch'Anfïon dal duro monte
tirò li sassi al bel muro dirceo;
o qual d'intorn'al fonte pegaseo
cantâr più bel color che già la fronte
s'ornâr d'alloro, con le Muse conte
uomo lodando, o forse alcuno deo,

sarebbe scarso a commendar costei,
le cui bellezze assai più che mortali
ed i costumi e le parole sono.
Ed io presumo in versi diseguali
di disegnarle in canto senza suono!
Vedete s'e' son folli i pensier' miei!

37

Bright pristine oriental pearls beneath
vivacious rubies rose and crimson red
from which angelic laughter is expressed
that frequently makes Jove and Venus shine
together underneath two black eyelashes,
and making up her colour everywhere
white lilies mixed with roses scarlet red
without a trace of any artifice:

her golden curly locks are radiant
above her lovely brow, by which the god
of Love is overwhelmed with wonderment;
and all her other features harmonize
in equal measure with the prior traits,
so that she bears the likeness of true angels.

38

That pleasant song with which once Orpheus
tamed Cerberus and the Acheron's steersman,
or that with which Amphion carted stones
from the hard cliff to the fair wall of Dirce;
or that which those who once adorned their brow
with laurel sang near the Pegasian spring
more beautifully in praising man, beside
the skillful Muses, or perhaps some god,

would be inadequate to honour her,
whose beauty, bearing, and whose eloquence
are so much greater than what mortals vaunt.
And I presume to illustrate these traits
in silent verses that aren't adequate!
Consider now how foolish are my thoughts!

39

Scrivon alcun' Partenopè, sirena
ornata di bellezze e piena d'arte,
aver sua stanza eletta in questa parte
tra il coll'erboso e la marina rena,
e qui lasciat'ancor d'età non piena
le membra sua, che or son cener' sparte,
e il nome suo in più felice carte
e in questa terra fertile e amena.

E com'a le' fu il ciel mite e benigno,
così alle poi nate par ch'e' sia:
ed io, miser a me!, sovente il provo
veggendo bella la nemica mia
vincer ogni mia forza col suo ingegno,
ver' me mostrando sempre sdegno novo.

40

Dice con meco l'anima tal volta:
"Come potevi tu già mai sperare
che dove Bacco può quel che vuol fare,
e Cerere v'abbonda in copia molta,
e dove fu Partenopè sepolta,
ov'ancor le sirene uson cantare,
amor, fede, onestà potesse stare
o fosse alcuna sanità raccolta?

E stu 'l vedevi, come t'occuparo
i fals'occhi di questa che non t'ama
e la qual tu con tanta fede segui?
Dèstati omai, e fuggi il lito avaro!
fuggi colei che la tua morte brama!
Che fai? che pensi? ché non ti dilegui?".

39

Some say Partenope, the siren decked
with loveliness and full of craftiness,
desired to settle in this area
between the grassy hill and sandy coast,
and at a tender age leave her remains
nearby, which are now ashes strewn about,
and leave her name on many treasured pages
and in this fertile and alluring land.

As heaven was benign and good to her,
it seems it is to women born here too:
and I, alas for me!, am often proof of this
in seeing my lovely enemy prevail
against my forces with her cleverness,
by always showing me renewed disdain.

40

From time to time my soul will say to me:
"How is it that you ever could have hoped
that where both Bacchus does just what he wants
and Ceres is profusely plentiful,
and where Partenope was laid to rest,
where still the sirens are inclined to sing,
love, faith, and honesty could ever dwell
or any sanity be found at all?

And if you know this, how did the false eyes
of one who does not love you conquer you,
one whom you follow after faithfully?
Wake up, now, flee the shore of greediness!
Flee her who only yearns to see you die!
What are you doing? thinking? why not steal away?"

41

Chi che s'aspetti con piacer i fiori
e di verde le piante rivestire
e per le selve gli uccelletti udire
cantando forse i lor più caldi amori,
io non son quel; ma, com'io sento fuori
Zefiro e veggio il bel tempo venire,
così m'attristo: e parmi allor sentire
nel petto un duol, il qual par che m'accuori.

Ed è di questo Baia la cagione,
la qual invita sì col suo diletto
colei che là sem-porta la mia pace
che non me l' fa alcun'altra stagione.
E che io vadia là mi è interdetto
da lei, che può di me quel che le piace.

42

Intra 'l Barbaro monte e 'l mar Tirreno
sied'il lago d'Averno intornïato
da calde fonti, e dal sinistro lato
gli sta Pozzuolo, ed a destro Miseno;
il qual sent'ora ogni suo grembo pieno
di belle donne, avendo racquistato
le frondi, la verdura e 'l tempo ornato
di feste, di diletto e di sereno.

Questi con la bellezza sua mi spoglia
ogn'anno, nella più lieta stagione,
di quella donna ch'è sol mio desire.
A sé la chiama; ed io, contra mia voglia,
rimango senza il cuore, in gran quistione
qual men dorriemi, il viver o 'l morire.

41

One looking forward with delight to flowers
in bloom and plants reclothed once more in green
and hearing little birds throughout the woods
sing songs, perhaps about their fondest loves,
that one's not me; but, feeling Zephyrus
outside and seeing warm weather has arrived,
I grow forlorn: and then I seem to feel
a pain inside my breast that breaks my heart.

And Baia is the reason for this pain,
a place so beautiful that it attracts
the lady who bears with her all my peace,
which she in other seasons does not do.
I am prohibited from going there
by her, who can do with me what she wants.

42

Avernus lies between the mountain peak
of Barbaro and the Tyrrhenian Sea
surrounded by hot springs, and to its left
sits Pozzuolo, to its right Misenum;
it shows that every valley is now full
of lovely women, having reacquired
its foliage, its leafy boughs, and time
of gaiety, of pleasure and clear skies.

Every year its beauty makes me feel,
throughout the fairest season, left stripped bare
of her, the only one whom I desire.
It calls to her; and I, against my will,
am left without my heart, and questioning
which would cause me less pain, my life or death.

43

Toccami 'l viso Zefiro tal volta
più che l'usato alquanto impetüoso,
quasi sé stesso allora avesse schiuso
dal cuoi' d'Ulisse, e la catena sciolta.
E poi che l'alma tutt'ha in sé raccolta,
par ch'e' mi dica: "Leva il volto suso:
mira la gioia ch'io, da Baia effuso,
ti porto in questa nuvola rinvolta".

Io lievo gli occhi: e parmi tanto bella
veder madonna entr'a quell'aura starse
che 'l cor vien men sol nel maravigliarse.
E com'io veggio lei più presso farse,
lievomi per pigliarla e per tenella:
e 'l vento fugge, ed essa spare in quella.

44

E Cinzïo e Caucàso, Ida e Sigeo,
Libano, Séna, Carmelo ed Ermone,
Athòs, Olimpo, Pindar, Citerone,
Aracinto, Menàlo, Ismo e Rifeo,
Etna, Pachin, Peloro e Lilibeo,
Vesevo, Gaür, Massich'e Caulone,
Apennin, l'Alpi, Balbo e Borïone,
Atlante, Abila, Calpe e Pireneo,

o qualunqu'altro monte, ombre giammai
ebber cotanto grate a' lor pastori
quant'a me furon quelle di Miseno;
nelle quai sì benigno Amor trovai
che refrigerio diede a' mia ardori
ed ad ogni mia noia pose freno.

43

At times Zephyrus blows against my face
with somewhat greater force than usual,
as he did when he had unloosed himself
from Ulysses's wineskins, and then escaped.
And after having captured my whole soul,
he seems to say to me: "Lift up your eyes:
gaze on the joy that I, breathed here from Baia,
bring to you enveloped in this cloud."

I lift my eyes and seem to see my love
supported by the air so beautifully
my heart succumbs just from its wonderment.
And as I see her coming nearer me,
I rise to grasp her and hold on to her:
the wind then flees, and vanishes with her.

44

Caucasia, Cinto, Ida and Sigeum,
Lebanon and Sinai, Carmel, Hermon,
Olympus, Athos, Pindus, Cithaeron,
Aracynthus, Menelaus, the Isthmus, Ripheus,
Etna, Pachynus, Faro, and Marsala,
Vesuvius, Gaurus, Massicus, Caulon,
the Apennines, Alps, Balbus, Borion,
the Pyrenees, Abyla, Atlas, Calpe,

or any other mountain, never pleased
its shepherds with so great a ring of shade
as did Misenum's in delighting me;
I found there Love, who was so welcoming
he brought relief to my intense desires
and put an end to all my suffering.

45

Colui per cui, Misen, primieramente
foste nomato, cui cenere ancora
sparte nella tua terra fan dimora
– e faran, credo, perpetüalmente –,
facea trombando inanimar la gente
ed ad arme ed a guerra, d'ora in ora,
e de' legni d'Enea di poppa in prora
batter il mar co' remi virilmente.

Ma tu di pace e d'amor e di gioia
sei fatto grembo e dilettoso seno,
degno d'eterno nome e di memoria.
Ben lo so io, ch'in te ogni mia noia
lasciai, e femmi d'allegrezza pieno
colui ch'è sire e re d'ogni mia gloria.

46

Se io temo di Baia e il cielo e il mare,
la terra e l'onde e i laghi e le fontane
e le parti domestiche e le strane,
alcun non se ne dèe maravigliare.
Quivi s'attende solo a festeggiare
con suoni e canti, e con parole vane
ad inveschiar le menti non ben sane,
o d'Amor le vittorie a ragionare.

Ed havvi Vener sì piena licenza
che spess'avvien che tal Lucrezia vienvi
che torna Clëopatra allo suo ostello.
Ed io lo so, e di quinci ho temenza
non con la donna mia sì fatti siènvi,
che 'l petto l'aprino ed ìntrinsi in quello.

45

Misenum, he from whom you took your name
at birth, the one whose scattered ashes still
are found to have their dwelling on your land
– and will, I think, in perpetuity –
would thrill the people with his trumpet's sounds
with calls to arms and war, from time to time,
and would propel Aeneas's ships at sea
by rowing bravely at both stern and prow.

But you are made of gulfs and pleasant bays
of placidness and love and joyfulness,
whose name and memory deserve to last.
I know full well that all my pain I left
with you, and was made full of joy by him
who is the lord and king of all my fame.

46

If I'm upset by Baia's sky and sea,
its shore, its waves, its hot springs and its lakes,
its places both familiar and unknown,
no one should be in any way surprised.
Here people just expect to celebrate
by making noise and singing, and seduce
with empty words the minds of those less chaste,
or talk about their victories with Love.

The freedom Venus plies there is so great
that often one arrives as a Lucrece
and as a Cleopatra goes back home.
And knowing this, I consequently fear
my lady might be stirred by things like these
such that they breach her heart and enter it.

47

Perir possa il tuo nome, Baia, e il loco,
boschi selvaggi le tua piagge sièno,
e le tue fonti diventin veneno,
né vi si bagni alcun molto né poco;
in pianto si converta ogni tuo gioco,
e suspetto diventi el tuo bel seno
a' naviganti; il nuvolo e 'l sereno
in te riversin fumo, solfo e fuoco:

ché hai corrotto la più casta mente
che fosse 'n donna, con la tua licenza,
se 'l ver mi disser gli occhi non è guari.
Laond'io sempre viverò dolente,
come ingannato da folle credenza;
or foss'io stato cieco non ha guari!

48

Le nevi sono, e le piogge, cessate,
l'ira del ciel, le nebbie e le freddure;
i fior', le frondi e le fresche verdure,
i lieti giorni e le feste tornate.
Le donne son più che l'usato ornate,
e tutte quasi Amor le crëature
trastulla e mena per le sue pasture,
nel nuovo tempo, credo, innamorate.

Per ch'io conosco ciò ch'io non vorrei:
a Baia esser colei 'n sé no<n> invita
che muove e gira tutti e disir' miei.
Or dormiss'io infino alla reddita,
o girmene potessi là con lei,
o non saper ch'ella vi fosse ita!

47

May your name perish, Baia, with your town,
and wilderness replace your countryside,
your fountain waters become venomous,
and no one bathe there often or at all;
may all your joy be turned to bitterness,
your lovely gulf become a source of fear
for mariners; from clear or cloudy skies
may lightning, smoke, and sulphur fall on you:

for you have corrupted the purest mind
found in a woman with your wantonness,
if my eyes recently have told the truth.
So I will always have a life of pain,
like one who's been deceived by foolish thought:
if only for so long I'd not been blind!

48

The falling snow and showers have now ceased,
and heaven's wrath, and fog and chilliness;
and flowers, foliage, new greenery,
and happy days and festive times are back.
The women are bedecked in finery,
and Love makes merry almost everyone
and leads them all about his meadowlands,
in the new season, I believe, in love.

Because of this I know what I'd not want:
for her who stirs and spurs all my desires
to be in Baia not unwillingly.
If only I could sleep till her return,
or if I could go there to be with her,
or even not know that she had gone there.

49

Per certo, quando il ciel con lieto aspetto
riguarda ver' la stagione novella,
nulla contrada ha 'l mondo così bella
né dove più si prenda di diletto.
Quivi Amor regna senz'alcun sospetto,
o 'l ciel che 'l faccia o singulare stella;
Venere credo poi venisse in quella,
del mare uscendo, come in luogo eletto.

Quivi le piagge, la marina, i prati
son pien' di donne e di leggiadri amanti,
e ciò che piac'e' par vi si conceda.
Quivi son feste e dilettosi canti;
quivi si mettono amorosi agguati,
né mai senza gioir si leva preda.

50

Chi non credrà assai agevolmente
– s'al canto d'Arïon venne il delfino
faccendo sé al suo legno vicino,
al suo comando presto ed ubidiente –
che, solcando costei il mar sovente
in breve barca, nel tempo più fino,
alla voce del suo canto divino
molti ne venghin desïosamente?

E quas'a ciò da Nettunno mandati,
circondan quella, e ogni cosa sinéstra
cacciando indrieto, e onde e tempestate.
O orecchi felici, o cuor' beati,
a' quali è la Fortuna tanto destra
che d'ascoltarla fatti degni siate!

49

Most certainly when the fair sky regards
the new season with joyous happiness,
no territory is so beautiful
and nowhere else is more enjoyable.
Here Love holds sway without the least concern,
of either heaven or of any star;
and I believe that Venus then came there,
and, having left the sea, made it her home.

Here the marina, beaches, and the leas
abound with women and their graceful beaus,
and it seems all can find there what they wish.
Here there are festas and delightful songs;
here amorous ensnarements are devised,
and seizing prey will always lead to joy.

50

Who would not very easily believe
– if at the song of Arion the dolphin
came and drew itself close to his boat,
obeying his express command with haste –
that, sailing often in a little boat
across the waters of the sea, in spring,
the heavenly sound of her melodies
would draw so many yearningly to her?

And almost as if Neptune sent them there,
they circle her, and all that's sinister
they drive away from her, both waves and storms.
O happy ears indeed, O blissful hearts,
to which Fortune has been so favourable
that you have been made worthy to hear her.

51

Su la poppa sedea d'una barchetta,
che 'l mar segando presta era tirata,
la donna mia con altre acompagnata,
cantando or una or altra canzonetta.
Or questo lito ed or quest'isoletta,
ed ora questa ed or quella brigata
di donne visitando, era mirata
qual discesa dal cielo un'angioletta.

Io, che, seguendo lei, vedeva farsi
da tutte parti incontro a rimirarla
gente, vedea come miracol nuovo.
Ogni spirito mio in me destarsi
sentiva, e con amor di commendarla
sazio non vedea mai il ben ch'io provo.

52

Guidommi Amor, ardendo ancora il sole,
sopra l'acque di Giulio, in un mirteto,
ed era il mar tranquillo e il ciel quïeto,
quantunque alquanto Zefir, com'e' suole,
movesse agli arbuscei le cime sole:
quando mi parve udire un canto, lieto
tanto, che simil non fu consüeto
d'udir già mai nelle mortali scuole.

Per ch'io: "Angela forse, o ninfa, o dea
canta con seco in questo loco eletto,
– meco diceva – degli antichi amori".
Quinci madonna in assai bel ricetto
del bosco ombroso, in su l'erbe e in su' fiori,
vid'i' cantando, e con altre sedea.

51

My lady sat accompanied by friends
beside the tiller of a little boat
that swiftly sped across the open sea,
while singing this and then another song.
Now stopping on this isle and then that shore,
and visiting for company one group
of ladies, then another, she appeared
to be an angel who'd come down from heaven.

And I, who, in her wake, saw people come
from everywhere to gaze upon her, saw
her as if she were a new miracle.
I felt my spirits, every one of them,
awake, and with the love of praising her,
I never saw the good I felt expire.

52

Love guided me, the sun still blazing hot,
across the Julian gulf, the sea at rest,
the sky serene, into a myrtle grove,
though Zephyrus somewhat, as usual,
moved just the top boughs of the sapling trees,
when I seemed then to hear a lovely voice
in song unlike I'd ever heard before
at any music school where mortals sing.

Thus I: "An angel, nymph, or deity
perhaps is singing to herself" – I thought –
"within this grove reserved for ancient loves."
And there my lady, in a lovely copse
inside the shaded woods, by grass and flowers,
was singing, as I saw, beside her friends.

53

Il Cancro ardea, passata la sest'ora,
spirava Zefiro e il tempo era bello,
quïeto il mar, e in su lito di quello,
in parte dove il sol non era ancora
vid'io colei che 'l ciel di sé innamora
en più donne far festa: e l'aureo véllo
le cingea 'l capo in guisa che capello
del vago nodo non usciva fuora.

Neptuno, Glauco, Forco e la gran Teti
dal mar lei riguardavan sì contenti
che dir parevon: "Giove, altro non voglio!".
Ïo, da un ronchio, fissi agli occhi lieti,
sì adoppiati aveva e sentimenti
ch'un sasso paravamo io e lo scoglio.

54

Iscinta e scalza, con le trezze avvolte,
e d'uno scoglio in altro trapassando,
conche marine da quelli spiccando,
giva la donna mia con altre molte.
E l'onde, quasi in sé tutte raccolte,
con picciol moto i bianchi piè bagnando,
innanzi si spingevan mormorando
e ritraensi iterando le volte.

E se tal volta, forse di bagnarsi
temendo, i vestimenti in sù tirava,
sì ch'io vedeo più della gamba schiuso,
oh, quali avria veduto allora farsi,
chi rimirato avesse dov'io stava,
gli occhi mia vaghi di mirar più suso!

53

The Crab was blazing hot, the sext now past,
and Zephyrus was blowing and the sky
was clear, the sea at rest, and on its shore,
just where the sun had not yet reached,
I saw the one who makes the sky love her
in merriment with many of her friends:
her golden veil was wrapped about her head
so that it covered up her braided hair.

Neptune, Glaucus, Phorcys, and great Tethys
were gazing on her from the sea, so pleased
they seemed to say: "Jove, this is all I want!"
Upon a cliff, fixed on her lovely eyes,
I found my senses to be so benumbed
the cliff and I appeared to be one stone.

54

Barefoot, scantly dressed, her hair in braids,
passing over one rock to the next,
collecting seashells from the tidal pools,
my lady walked along with many friends.
And as if piling on themselves, the waves,
submerging her white feet in little swirls,
propelled themselves ahead while murmuring
and then receded many times in turn.

And if at times she pulled her clothing up,
afraid perhaps it might become all wet,
so that I saw more of her leg revealed,
oh, what would someone then expect to see,
were they to gaze from where I was,
my eyes desiring to gaze higher up!

55

O dì felice, o ciel chiaro sereno,
o prati, o arbuscegli, o dolci amori,
o angeliche voci, o lieti cori,
de' qual' vidi un bel giardin ripieno;
o celeste armonia, la qual seguièno
non so s'i' dica angelichi splendori
o vergini terrene, e tra ' be' fiori
e le piante danzando si movièno!

Chi con istile ornato e con preciso
discriver' ne potrïa le vedute
bellezze, mai non viste fra' mortali?
Non io, ch', esser credendo in paradiso,
muover sentiï secreta virtute
che 'l cor m'aprì con più di mille strali.

56

D'oro crespi capelli ed annodati
da sé, da verde frondi e bianchi fiori,
un angelico viso e due splendori
simili a stelle, e atti non usati
veder fra noi, vezzosi e riposati,
ed un cantar di più gioiosi amori
söave e lieto ben tra mille fiori
del primo tempo, insieme radunati

in un giardino nato ad un bel fonte,
pos'Amore in amare alla mia mente
libera ancora, semplice e leggera.
Né pria, dal canto desto, alza' la fronte,
che tutte l'accerchiâr subitamente;
e presa, a lui la dier, che vicin era.

55

O happy day, O sky serene and bright,
O meadows, sapling trees, O sweetest loves,
O angelic voices, O delightful choirs,
of which I saw a lovely garden rife;
O celestial harmony, in tow
angelic splendours, maybe earthly virgins,
I cannot say, and among lovely flowers
and plants, all moved together in a dance.

Who could describe the beauty of this scene
with clarity and in an ornate style,
a beauty never seen by mortal souls?
Not I, who, thinking it was paradise,
began to feel a secret power move
that opened up my heart with scores of shafts.

56

Her wavy golden hair tied back upon
itself, with twigs of green leaves and white flowers,
an angel's countenance and two bright lights
that shine like stars, a bearing never seen
among us, beautiful and dignified,
and songs about the most enchanting loves,
serene and jubilant among a mass of flowers
of the first season, brought together in

a garden grown beside a lovely spring,
Love placed, for me to love, within my mind
which was still free, light-hearted, and relaxed.
The singing woke me, and no sooner did
I lift my head than all this circled it;
and seized, they gave it to him, who stood near.

57

Intorn'ad una fonte, in un pratello
di verdi erbette pieno e di bei fiori,
sedean tre angiolette, i loro amori
forse narrando, e a ciascuna 'l bello
viso adombrava un verde ramicello
ch'i capei d'òr cingea, al qual di fuori
e d'entro insieme i dua vaghi colori
avolgeva un süave venticello.

E dopo alquanto l'una alle due disse
(com'io udi'): "Deh, se, per avventura,
di ciascuna l'amante or qui venisse,
fuggiremo noi quinci per paura?".
A cui le due risposer: "Chi fuggisse,
poco savia saria, co·tal ventura!".

58

All'ombra di mill'arbori fronzuti,
in abito leggiadro e gentilesco,
con gli occhi vaghi e col cianciar donnesco
lacci tendea, da lei prima tessuti
de' suoi biondi capei crespi e soluti
al vento lieve, in prato verde e fresco,
un'angiolella; a' quai giungeva vésco
tenace Amor, ed ami aspri e acuti.

Da' quai chi v'incappava, lei mirando,
invan tentava poi lo svilupparsi,
tant'era l'artificio che i teneva.
Ed io lo so, che me di me fidando
più che 'l dovere, infra e lacciuoli sparsi
fui preso da virtù ch'io non vedeva.

57

Beside a spring, upon a narrow lea
of verdure overspread with lovely flowers,
sat three young little angels, speaking of
those whom they loved, perhaps, and a green sprig
lent shade to each of their fair faces, sprigs
that ringed their golden hair, outside of which
as well as inside a soft gentle breeze
was folding the two colours into one.

And sometime later one said to her two
companions (as I heard): "Ah, if by chance
each of our lovers were to come here now,
would we then flee because we felt afraid?"
To which the other two replied: "The one
who fled would not be wise, with luck like that!"

58

Beneath the shade of countless leafy trees,
attired in graceful and exquisite clothes,
with lovely eyes and speaking graciously,
an angel stretched a snare, which she first spun
from her blonde curly hair borne by a breeze
of gentle air, upon a fresh green lawn;
to which the strong-willed god of Love applied
his charm, as well as sharp and pointed hooks.

Whoever stumbled there, observing her,
would try in vain to liberate himself,
so strong was the device which gripped him fast.
And this I know, for, trusting myself more
than I should have, among the traps strewn there,
I was seized by a force I did not see.

59

Non credo il suon tanto söave fosse
che gli occhi d'Argo tutti fé dormire;
né d'Anfïon la citara a udire
quando li monti a chiuder Tebe mosse;
né le sirene ancor, quando si scosse
invano Ulisse provido al fuggire,
né altro, se alcun se ne può dire
forse più dolce, o di più alte posse:

quant'una voce ch'io d'un'angioletta
udi', che lieta i suoi biondi capelli
cantand'ornava di frond' e di fiori.
Quindi nel petto entrommi una *fiammetta*,
la qual, mirando li sua occhi belli,
m'accese il cor in più di mill'ardori.

60

Levasi il sol tal volta in orïente
senz'alcun raggio e rosso pe' vapori;
la luna, maculata di colori
oscuri, appar men bella e men lucente;
e del cielo ne sono assai sovente
dalle nuvole tolti gli splendori;
e ' nostri lumi, vie molto minori,
per poco vento diventan nïente.

Ma que' begli occhi splendidi, ne' quali
Amor fabrica e tempra le saette
che mi passano il core a tutte l'ore,
nebbia né vento curan, ma son tali
quai furon sempre: due vive *fiammette*,
lucenti più ch'alcuno altro splendore.

59

I don't believe the sound that made the eyes
of Argus fall asleep was quite as sweet;
nor was Amphion's lyre while he played
when he moved mountains to encircle Thebes;
nor, likewise, was the sirens' singing when
in vain Ulysses woke prepared to flee,
nor any other, if it can be said
to be perhaps more powerful or sweet,

as was a little angel's voice I heard,
one who was decorating her blonde hair
with leaves and flowers while singing happily.
Then in my breast there came a *little flame*,
which, as I gazed into her lovely eyes,
inflamed my heart with myriad desires.

60

At times the sun ascending in the east
cannot be seen and through the fog looks red;
the moon, its surface spotted with dark hues,
appears less lovely and less luminous;
and very often in the sky the clouds
will cause the stars to disappear from view;
and our own lights, being many times less strong,
can be blown out by just a little breeze.

But those refulgent lovely eyes, in which
Love fabricates and tempers all his darts
that unremittingly pass through my heart,
show no concern for wind or fog, but are
as they have always been: two living *flames*,
more lucent than all other shining lights.

61

Il mar tranquillo, producer la terra
fiori e erbette, el ciel queto girarsi,
gli uccelli più che l'usato allegrarsi,
quando fuori Eöl Zefiro disserra,
ho già veduto. Se 'l veder non erra,
vegg'io le donne belle e vaghe farsi,
e le bestie ne' boschi accompagnarsi,
e pace e triegua farsi d'ogni guerra,

posarsi buoi delle fatiche loro,
e ' bobolchi e ' pastor' sotto alcuna ombra
cercare il fresco e riposarsi alquanto.
Ma io, che per amor mi discoloro
e cui disio più che speranza ingombra,
riposare non posso tanto o quanto.

62

Chi crederia giammai ch'esser potesse
nel cuor d'una gran *fiamma* il ghiaccio ascoso?
Chi crederebbe ch'è quel poderoso
che petto alcun come foco accendesse?
Chi crederia che la *fiamma* facesse
tremar alcun, quantunque paüroso?
Chi crederia che 'l freddo aspro e noioso
a furia alcun per sua forza movesse?

Crederoll'io, che dentro al petto mio,
quando sdegnosa questa *fiamma* fassi,
sento l'alma tremar e farsi fredda;
e sì m'affuoca, quando vo, che io
temo di cener farmi. Ed ella stassi
com ghiaccio all'ombra o neve in parte stretta.

61

The sea serene, the soil producing flowers
and grass, the heavens turning silently,
the birds more joyful than is usual,
when Aeolus releases Zephyrus,
I have already seen. If my sight's true,
then I see women beautifying themselves,
and animals out mating in the woods,
and all wars finding peace and armistice,

and oxen resting from their labouring,
and peasants and farmworkers seeking out
cool air beneath some shade and finding rest.
But I, however, who grow pale from love
and am suffused more by desire than hope,
cannot find rest of any kind at all.

62

Who'd ever think some hidden ice could find
itself inside the heart of a great *flame*?
Who'd ever think it was so powerful
that it could set someone ablaze like fire?
Who would believe that any *flame* could make
a person shake, however prone to fear?
Who would believe a harsh annoying cold
could have the strength to make someone go mad?

I would believe it since within my heart,
each time this *flame* becomes contemptuous,
I feel my soul then tremble and grow cold;
and it sets me on fire, when I'm with her,
so much I fear I'll turn to ash. And she's
like ice in shade or snow in a recess.

63

Come in sul fonte fu preso Narcisso
di sé da sé, così costei, specchiando
sé, sé ha preso dolcemente amando.
E tanto vaga sé stessa vagheggia
che, ingelosita della sua figura,
ha di chïunque la mira paura,
temendo sé a sé non esser tolta.
Quel che ella di me pensi, colui
se l' pensi che in sé conosce altrui.

A me ne par, per quel ch'appar di fore,
qual fu tra Febo e Danne, odio e amore.

64

Infra l'eccelso coro d'Elicona
mi transportò l'altr'ieri il mio ardire;
là dove, attento standomi ad udire
ciò che in quel s'adopra e si ragiona,
vidi, qual forse già fu la lacona
donna di Paris, una ninfa uscire
d'un lieto bosco e verso me venire
co' crin' ristretti da verde corona.

A me venuta disse: "Io son colei
che fo di chi mi segue il nome eterno,
e qui venuta sono ad amar presta;
lieva sù, vieni!". Ed io, già di costei
acceso, mi levai: ond'io, d'inferno
uscendo, entrai nell'amorosa festa.

63

As at the well Narcissus was possessed
of himself by himself, so, looking at
herself, she sweetly took herself to love.
And she looks on herself so lovingly
that, having become jealous of her form,
she is afraid of everybody's gaze,
for fear of being taken from herself.
Whatever she should feel for me, let him
imagine he knows others in himself.

It's evident to me it's like the case
of Phoebus and Daphne, of love and hate.

64

The other day my ardour carried me
up to the lofty choir of Helicon,
where, listening attentively to what
was being done and what was being said,
I saw, perhaps, one whom once Paris loved,
the lady from Laconia, a nymph,
come forward towards me from a pleasant grove,
her tresses gathered by a crown of green.

She came to me and said: "I am the one
who makes the names of those who follow me
eternal, and I've come prepared to love.
Arise and come with me!" Already being
inflamed by her, I rose; and leaving hell,
I came into a festival of love.

65

Sovra li fior' vermigli e ' capei d'oro
veder mi parve un foco alla Fiammetta
e quel mutarsi in una nugoletta
lucida più che mai argento od oro.
E qual candida perla in anel d'oro,
tal si sedeva in quella un'angioletta,
voland'al cielo splendida e soletta,
d'orïental zafir vestita e d'oro.

Io m'allegrai, alte cose sperando,
dov'io dovea conoscer che a Dio
in breve era madonna per salire,
com'e' poi fu: ond'io qui, lagrimando,
rimaso sono in doglia e in desio
di morte per potere a lei salire.

66

Vetro son fatti i fiumi, ed i ruscelli
gli serra di fuor ora la freddura;
vestiti son i monti e la pianura
di bianca neve e nudi gli arbuscelli,
l'erbette morte, e non cantan gli uccelli
per la stagion contraria a lor natura;
Borëa soffia, e ogni crëatura
sta chiusa per lo freddo ne' sua ostelli.

Ed io, dolente, solo ardo ed incendo
in tanto foco che quel di Vulcano
a rispetto non è una favilla;
e giorno e notte chiero, a giunta mano,
alquanto d'acqua al mio signor, piangendo,
né ne posso impetrar sol una stilla!

65

Above the crimson flowers and curls of gold
a fire encircling Fiammetta appeared
and changed itself into a little cloud
more radiant than silver or than gold.
And like a bright pearl in a ring of gold,
so was she sitting in it angel-like,
in flight towards heaven, shining and alone,
attired in oriental sapphire and in gold.

I then felt joy, expecting something great,
at which I came to realize that soon
my lady would ascend to be with God.
This came to pass: so I, being here below
and shedding tears, was left in agony,
desiring to ascend and be with her.

66

The rivers have become all glass, the cold
has now sealed up the surface of the streams;
the mountains and the plains are covered up
with pure white snow and all the trees are bare,
the grass is dead, and birds no longer sing
because the season's hostile to their kind;
Boreas blows, and every creature stays
inside its dwelling owing to the cold.

Yet I, in pain, alone am roused and burn
inside a fire so great that Vulcan's own
is not a spark when it's compared to mine;
and day and night, with folded hands, I beg
my lord, while weeping, for a bit of water,
but I cannot obtain a single drop!

67

Pervenut'è insin nel secul nostro
che tante volte il cuor di Prometèo
con l'altre parti dentro si riféo,
di quante se n' pascé un duro rostro.
Il che parria forse terribil mostro,
se non fêsse di me simil trofeo
sovent'Amor, ch'a scriverlo potéo
far del mio lagrimar penna ed inchiostro.

Io piango, e sento ben che 'l cor si sface;
e allor, quand'egli è per venir meno,
debile, smunto e punto per l'affanno,
O Dio!, nascoso sento che 'l riface
el mio destin: läonde eterne fièno
le pene che mi dìsfano e rifanno.

68

Dietro al pastor d'Ameto alle materne
ombre scendea quel che ad Agenòre
furtò la figlia, quella il cui valore
nei mur' troiani ancora si discerne,
quando tal donna, quale ad Oloferne
con tristo augurio si arse il fero core,
m'apparve, accesa con quello splendore
che è terza luce nelle rote eterne:

e femmi tal, vezzosa riguardando,
qual fé Cupido la figlia di Belo,
stando ella attenta ed Enea ragionando.
Läond'io ardo; ed ardendo del gelo
che sentì Biblìs, temo, imaginando
che 'l vestir bruno ed il candido velo

non la faccia crudel ovvero onesta
oltre el disio che per lei mi molesta.

67

The legend has survived into our time
that, as often as Prometheus's heart
and all its inner parts have been remade,
so often did a hard beak feed on them.
And this would seem a frightening spectacle,
had Love not similarly often made
of me a trophy, so that he could have
composed it with my tears as pen and ink.

I weep and know full well my heart will break;
and then, just when it is about to faint,
being weak, worn out and wounded by distress,
O God!, I feel my hidden destiny
come back to life: so pain destroying me
and then remaking me will never cease.

68

Behind the shepherd of Admetus was
descending to the shades of Earth the one
who seized the daughter of King Agenor
whose merit's still seen on the Trojan walls,
when there appeared a woman, like the one
who captivated Holofernes's proud heart
portentously, inflamed with that bright light
which is the third of the eternal spheres:

she, looking charmingly at me, made me
like Cupid made the daughter of King Belus,
as she stood awestruck and Aeneas spoke.
And so I burn; and burning from the ice
that Byblis felt, I'm scared, imagining
that her dark dress and snow-white veil may make

her either cruel or virtuous beyond
my felt desire for her that pains me so.

69

Contento quasi ne' pensier' d'amore,
soletto un giorno in essi dimorava,
imaginando il suo alto valore.
E, mentre dolcemente più pensava,
Amor m'apparve con gioioso aspetto,
ver' me dicendo: "Qual pensier ti grava?
Non istar qui, ch'amoroso diletto
ti mosterrò, se tu mi seguirai,
di belle donne in fresco giardinetto".
Allora in piedi ritto mi levai,
seguendo lui, che diritto se n' gìo
in un giardin dilettevole assai.
Lasciommi quivi, e disse: "Mentre ch'io
a tornar penerò, fa' che m'aspetti";
e volando da me si dipartìo.
Ma e' non stette guari, ch'io vedetti
lui ritornar con dodici donzelle
gaie, leggiadre e con gentili aspetti.
Tutte eran fresche, dilicate e belle,
d'erbe e di frondi verdi coronate,
negli occhi lor lucenti più che stelle.
Tutte danzando venieno ordinate
su un bel prato d'erbette e di fiori,
nel qual danzando Amor l'avea menate.
Fêssi ver' me Amor: "Tu che di fori
della danza dimori, riguardando
ne' belli occhi a costoro i miei ardori,
odile nominare, sì che, quando
forse sarai di fuor da questo loco,
d'onorarle disii per mio comando.
Tra l'altre, che più guarda il nostro foco
con senno e con virtù costei è quella
allato a cui con allegrezza gioco:
di Giachinotto monna Itta s'appella,
de' Tornaquinci; e Meliana è colei,

69

Like one who's happy thinking about love,
alone one day I pondered over it,
reflecting on its worthy excellence.
And as I slowly gave it further thought,
Love with a joyful look appeared to me,
and said to me: "What thoughts weigh on your mind?
Do not stay here, I'll show you the delight,
if you will follow me, that love can bring
with lovely ladies in a pleasant garden."
I then rose to my feet to follow him,
who straight away departed, entering
a garden that was most agreeable.
He left me there, and said: "While my return
will be delayed somewhat, wait for me here";
and flying off he took his leave of me.
But it was hardly any time before
I saw him reappear with twelve young maidens,
so gay and graceful, and with noble mien.
They all were fresh, refined and beautiful,
with garlands made of grass and verdant leaves,
their eyes more lucent than the stars above.
They all were dancing ceremonially
upon a pleasant lawn of grass and flowers,
a place to which Love, dancing, had brought them.
Love made his way towards me: "You who remain
outside the dance, while looking at my ardour
within the lovely eyes of those in front
of you, now listen as I call their names,
so when you've left this area, perhaps,
you'll want to honour them by my command.
More than the others, she who guards our fire
with wisdom and with virtue is the one
beside us with whom I play merrily:
her name is Monna Itta di Giachinotto,
of the Tornaquinci; in her wake

di Giovanni di Nello, ch'è dop'ella.
E la Lisa e la Pecchia, che con lei
vengono appresso, amendune figliuole
di Rinier Marignan son saper dèi.
A nostra danza quinta è il tuo sole,
cioè quella Fiammetta che ti diede
con la saetta al cor, ch'ancor ti dole.
Ell'è più bella ch'altra, ma nol crede
chi non riguarda lei con gli occhi tuoi,
però che tanto avanti alcun non vede.
E la bella lombarda segue poi,
monna Vanna chiamata; e se tu guardi,
nulla più bella n'è con essonoi.
Di Filippozzo Filippa de' Bardi
séguita bella, e poi monna Lottiera
di Neron Nigi con söavi sguardi.
La Vanna di Filippo, Primavera
da tal conosci tu degna chiamata,
vedila poi seguir nostra bandiera.
Allato Nifi a lei vedi onorata
Sismonda di Francesco Baroncelli,
e poi, appresso lei, accompagnata
Niccolosa è di Tedice Manoelli
insieme appresso con Bartolomea
di Giovanni: Beatrice cre' s'appelli.
E ben che 'n fine della danza stea,
non è men bella, ma vien per riscossa,
come tu vedi"; e io ben lo vedea.
Tacquesi allora, e la danza fu mossa
sopra ' bei fiori e sotto verde fronda,
che a' raggi solar' toglieva possa.
Onde ciascuna di quella gioconda
e bella danza, gaia e leggiadretta,
a cantar cominciò, come seconda
questa leggiadra e bella canzonetta:

is Meliana, of Giovanni di Nello.
Then Lisa and Pecchia follow her,
and both of them are daughters of Rinier
Marignan, and this you need to know.
Your sun in our dance is the fifth,
I mean the Fiammetta who struck you
right through the heart, which still hurts, with a dart.
She is more beautiful than all the rest,
but one who doesn't see her with your eyes
demurs, for one can't see that far ahead.
The lovely one from Lombardy comes next,
called Monna Vanna; if you would observe,
you'll see there's none more beautiful with us.
The lovely Filippozzo Filippa
de' Bardi comes, then Monna Lottiera
di Neron Nigi with her gentle eyes.
Then Vanna di Filippo, Primavera
as she is aptly named by one you know,
you see her following our streaming flag.
Right next to her you see the highly praised
Sismonda di Francesco Baroncelli,
and after her, then, in her company
is Niccolosa di Tedice Manoelli
together with Bartolomea di
Giovanni: Beatrice I think she's called.
Though she stands at the back end of the dance,
she's no less lovely, but she holds last place,
as you can see"; and this I saw quite well.
Then he grew quiet, and the dance advanced
upon the flowers and beneath the trees,
which minimized the force of the sun's rays.
Then everyone in that fine cheerful dance,
each frolicsome and graceful to behold,
began to sing, as illustrated by
this elegant and charming little song:

70

"Amor, dolce signore,
che hai il nostro core
in tua balìa, per Dio, fanne contente!

Tu sè nostro signor caro e verace,
e noi così volemo;
tu sè colui che ne può render pace
nel gran disio ch'avemo:
però quanto potemo
preghian tua signoria
che 'n ver' di noi si porti umilemente.

Noi siam qui giovinette, e tu 'l ti sai,
che poca di grevezza
che noi sentiam ci par sentire assai:
però la tua grandezza
a chïunque la sprezza,
signor, fàlla sentire,
ch'a noi non cal, che siam tue veramente.

Fa' sentire a coloro il tuo valore
che si fanno chiamare
inamorati sanza farti onore:
ché, se tu fai provare
lor quanto tu puoi fare,
saranno inamorati,
e noi ti loderem più degnamente.

Noi ardiam tutte per la tua virtute
nel tuo cocente foco.
Perdio, mercé! deh, donaci salute
anzi che mutiam loco,
ché già a poco a poco
per te ci consumiamo,
se tu non ci soccorri tostamente!

70

"Sir Love, dear lord of ours,
you who possess our hearts
within your care, by God, make us content!

You are our dear as well as our true lord,
and this is as we wish;
you are the one who can provide us peace
for the desire we have:
and so with all our might
your lordship we entreat
to act with great humility towards us.

We who are here are young, and you well know,
the little bit of pain
that we feel can seem to be great to us:
so anyone who scorns
your greatness, lord, make them
see that they understand
we do not care, for we are truly yours.

Do make those understand your worthiness
who say that they're in love
yet don't show you the honour you deserve:
for if you make them feel
the power that you have,
then they will fall in love,
and we will praise you more deservedly.

We all burn owing to your potency
in your hot, searing fire.
Good God, have mercy! Ah, give us relief
before we change our place,
because now bit by bit
we ruin ourselves for you,
if you do not come quickly to our aid!

Fa, signor nostro, gli animi pietosi
degli nostri amadori;
raffrena alquanto i lor atti orgogliosi
con più aspri dolori
che non hanno ne' cori:
sì che la nostra pena
e' provi come noi chi non la sente.

Entra en gli orecchi, qui, ballata, avanti,
ad Amor nostro siri;
e come tu pietosamente canti
i nostri aspri martirî,
fa che pregando il giri
a darci tosto gioia,
prima che ei n'uccida crudelmente".

71

I' non ardisco di levar più gli occhi
inverso donna alcuna,
qualora i' penso quel che m'ha fatt'una.

Nissuno amante mai con fermo core
o con puro volere
donna servì, com'io servia costei;
e quando più fedele al suo valore
credia merito avere,
giovane novo fé signor di lei.
Ond'io, bassando gli occhi dico: "Omei!
Non ne mirar nissuna,
ché, come questa, forse inganna ognuna".

Make merciful our lovers' temperaments,
dear lord; and do restrain
their forceful acts of arrogance somewhat
with pain that's more severe
than they have in their hearts:
so those who haven't felt
our pain will feel it just the way we do.

Ballata, come into the ears of Love,
advance here to our lord;
and as you sing about our bitter pain
most mercifully, see that
through prayer you might move him
to quickly bring us joy,
before he cruelly brings about our death."

71

No longer do I dare lift up my eyes
to look at any woman,
whenever I think what one did to me.

No lover ever served with steadfast heart
or ever with pure will
a lady as I used to serve that one;
and when I was more faithful to her worth
and thought I'd gain reward,
she made a new young man her noble lord.
So lowering my eyes I said, "Alas!
Don't look at even one,
for, like this one, perhaps they all deceive."

72

Non so qual i' mi voglia:
o viver o morir, per minor doglia.

Morir vorre', ché 'l viver m'è gravoso
veggendomi per altri esser lasciato;
e morte non vorre', ché, trapassato,
più non vedre' il bel vis'amoroso
per cui piango, invidioso
di chi l'ha fatto suo e me ne spoglia.

73

Il fior che 'l valor perde,
da ch' e' già cade, mai non si rinverde.

Perduto ho il valor mio,
e mia bellezza non serà com'era:
però ch'è van disio
chi perde il tempo e acquistarlo spera.
Io non son primavera,
che ogni anno si rinnova e fassi verde.

Io maledico l'ora
che 'l tempo giovenil fuggir lassai;
fantina essendo ancora,
esser abbandonata non pensai.
Non se rallegra mai
chi 'l primo fior del primo amore perde.

Ballata, assai mi duole
che a me non lice di metterti in canto.
Tu sai che 'l mio cor vole
vivere con sospiri, doglia e pianto:
così farò fintanto
che 'l foco di mia vita giugna al verde.

72

I don't know what I want:
to live or else to die, to ease the pain.

I'd want to die, for living torments me
in seeing myself dismissed for someone else;
and I don't want to die, for, being dead,
I would no longer see her pleasing face;
so I weep, envying
the one who made it his and robs me of it.

73

The flower that's lost its strength,
once it has fallen, never blooms again.

I've lost my strength,
my beauty will not be what it once was:
it's a vain wish
to waste time hoping to recover it.
I am not spring,
which yearly is renewed and turns to green.

I curse the hour
I let my days of youth escape from me;
a young girl still,
I did not think that I would be forsaken.
Whoever's lost
the first love's first flower never finds true joy.

Ballata, I
regret I cannot put you into song
You know my heart
desires to live with sighing, pain, and tears:
so I'll do that
until the fire of my life expires.

74

L'oscure fami e i pelagi tirreni,
e pigri stagni e li fiumi correnti,
mille coltella e gl'incendi cocenti,
le travi e i lacci e 'nfiniti veneni,
l'orribil rupi e ' massi e ' boschi pieni
di crude fere e di malvagie genti
vegnon, chiamate da' sospir' dolenti,
e mille modi da morire osceni.

E par ciascun mi dica: "Vienne, ch'io
son per iscaprestarti in un momento
da quel dolor nel quale Amor t'invischia!".
Ond'io a molti incontro col desio
talor mi fo, com'uom che n'ho talento;
ma poi la vita trista non s'arrischia.

75

Ipocràte, Avicenna o Galïeno,
dïamante, zafir, perla o rubino,
brettonica, marrobbio o rosmarino,
psalmo, evangelio ed orazion vie meno;
piova né vento, nuvol né sereno,
mago né negromante né indovino,
tartaro né giudeo né saracino,
né povertà né doglia, ond'io son pieno,

poteron mai del mio petto cacciare
questo rabbioso spirito d'amore
ch'a poco a poco alla morte mi tira.
Ond'io non so che mi debba sperare;
ed ei d'ogn'altro affan mi caccia fuore,
e, com'e' vuol, m'affligge e mi martira.

74

The painful hunger, the Tyrrhenian depths,
the stagnant pools, the rivers flowing fast,
the thousand knives, the incandescent fires,
the beams, the bonds, the countless poisoned cups,
the daunting cliffs, the rocks, the thickets full
of savage beasts and evil human beings
come to my mind, called forth by painful sighs,
and many, many brutal ways to die.

Each seems to say to me: "Come now, for I
can liberate you in a moment from
the pain in which Love has entangled you!"
So sometimes with desire I'll think about
the many ways, like one who's wishing to;
but then he won't risk his unhappy life.

75

Hippocrates, Avicenna, or Galen,
diamonds, sapphires, pearls or rubies,
betony, rosemary, or horehound,
the psalms, the gospels, speeches even less;
wind or rain, cloudy or clear skies,
magicians, necromancers, fortune tellers,
a Tartar, or a Jew or Saracen,
or poverty or pain, of which I'm full,

will never have the power to rid my heart
of this excruciating spirit of love
which gradually consigns me to my death.
So I don't know what hope I ought to have;
and it drives every other grief away,
and, as it wants, it racks and martyrs me.

76

Grifon', lupi, lëon', bisce e serpenti,
draghi, leopardi, tigri, orsi e cinghiari,
disfrenati cavai, tori armentari,
rabbiosi can', tempeste e discendenti
fólgori, tuoni, impetüosi venti,
rüine, incendi, scherani e corsari,
discorridori armati e sagittari
soglion fuggir le paürose genti.

Ma io, che non son tal, perché discerno
com'orribil fuggirmi a chi non torna,
fuggita, se non vede dipartirme?
Forse son io el diavol dell'inferno?
E crederrêl s'io avessi le corna,
poiché così a costei vegg'io fuggirme!

77

Perché ver' me pur dispermenti invano,
Amor, ché più de' tuoi esser non deggio?
Altro mar ti conviene, altro pileggio
cercar che 'l mio, da te fatto sì strano.
Ben puo' veder ch'ïo son fatto sano,
né tua mercé più non disio né chieggio;
e quanto più ti sforzi a farmi peggio,
tanto da te più mi truovo lontano.

Spent'è la *fiamma*, che m'accese ed arse,
fuggiti sono i mia giovini anni,
e tu co' modi tuo m'ha' fatto saggio.
Dunque, le tue saette invano sparse
ricogli omai, e sèrvati l'inganni
ad uccel nuovo, ch'io provati l'aggio.

76

Gryphons, wolves, lions, serpents, snakes,
dragons, leopards, tigers, bears and boars,
unbridled horses, herds of roaming bulls,
rabid dogs, and storms and lightning bolts
descending, and loud thunder, raging winds,
destruction, fires, bandits, privateers,
assaults by men with weapons and with bows
are things that fearful people tend to flee.

But since I'm not like that, why do I see
one flee me as if I were vile, who won't
return unless she sees that I'm not here?
Am I perhaps the devil come from hell?
If I were wearing horns I'd understand,
for then I'd know why she is fleeing me!

77

Why go on testing me in vain, lord Love,
when I no longer need to follow you?
Go search on other seas, on other routes
than mine, which you have made so alien.
For you can see quite well I've cured myself,
and I do not desire or seek your help;
the more you try to make it worse for me,
the more I separate myself from you.

The *flame* is spent, which burned and scalded me,
my tender years of youth are now long gone,
and you have made me wise to all your tricks.
So, go pick up the arrows you have shot
in vain, and save your underhanded tricks
for some young fool, for I have known them all.

78

Sì fuor d'ogni pensier nel qual ragione
passeggi o stia, seguendo l'appetito,
è il mio folle pensier del tutto uscito,
che paura nol può né riprensione,
né ancora colei che n'è cagione,
avendo il suo bel viso assai seguito,
ritrar dal corso, nel quale smarrito
corro all'ultima mïa destruzione.

Così fa, lasso!, negli anni migliori
il creder troppo al fervente desio
e l'invescarsi in le reti d'amore;
ché, quando vuol, non può poi degli errori
disvilupparsi il misero, che Dio
e sé offende, e vive male e muore.

79

Poco senn'ha chi crede la Fortuna
o con prieghi o con lacrime piegare,
e molto men chi crede lei fermare
con senno, con ingegno o arte alcuna.
Poco senn'ha chi crede atar la luna
a discorrer il ciel per suo sonare,
e molto men chi ne crede portare,
morendo, seco l'òr che qui raguna.

Ma più ch'altri mi par matto colui
ch'a femina, qual vogli, il suo onore,
sua libertà e la vita commette.
Elle donne non son, ma doglia altrui,
senza pietà, senza fé, senz'amore,
liete del mal di chi più lor credette.

78

My foolish mind has so completely gone
beyond the bounds of rationality
in all my thoughts by following desire
that neither fear nor censure, nor as well
the one who is the very cause of it,
my having so pursued her lovely face,
can hold it back upon the path where, lost,
I hasten towards my ultimate demise.

So does, alas, believing far too much
in passion's fervency during one's best years
and finding oneself tangled in love's net;
and even wanting to, in fact, the wretch
can't afterwards correct his faults, and thus
harms God and self, and wastes his life and dies.

79

Unwise is he who thinks that he can change
the tide of Fortune with appeals or tears,
and even less whoever thinks he will
inhibit it through wisdom, wit, or craft.
Unwise is he who thinks he helps the moon
move through the firmament by playing tunes,
and even less whoever thinks he can,
at death, take with him all his earthly wealth.

But maddest of them all, it seems to me,
is he who would entrust a woman, any,
with his honour, liberty, and life.
No, ladies they are not, but rather grief
to others, lacking pity, faith, or love,
content to harm those who put trust in them.

80a Ad Antonio Pucci

Due belle donne nella mente Amore
mi reca spesso: l'una delle quali
è di bellezze e di virtute eguali,
e l'altra, un poco di tempo maggiore.
Ma del vestir di ciascuna 'l colore
in abito la mostra diseguali:
per che mi dice parole cotali,
qual udirai appresso, 'l mio signore:

"Questa leggiadra e gaia giovinetta
pulzella è veramente; e l'altra poi,
di brun vestita, vedova dimora.
Ma, perché amar non possonsi a un'ora,
l'una convien ti sia donna per noi:
tosto di' quale amar più ti diletta".

In ciò da me non so prender consiglio:
però ricorro a te. Dimmi qual piglio?

80b Risposta di Antonio Pucci

Tu mi sei 'ntrato sì forte nel core
con le tue dolci rime naturali
che tutti i mie disiri temporali
son di servirti, e non d'altro tenore.
Ben ch'io d'ogn'esser sia di te minore,
com'io saprò, così ti dirò "Sali",
poiché Amor di sì fatti segnali
ti dice "Piglia qual ti par migliore".

Se 'nnanzi ch'e' sospinga la saetta
ti dà le prese ne' diletti tuoi,
prendi 'l vantaggio ed a poter l'onora.
Chi di fanciulla vergine innamora
con dubbio segue gli sembianti suoi,
però che rado attien quel che prometta.

Onde io ti dico, come a padre figlio,
che per la vedova abbandoni il giglio.

80a To Antonio Pucci

Two lovely ladies Love will often bring
into my mind, one of them equally
as beautiful as she is virtuous,
the other one being older by a bit.
But as to choice of clothing each prefers
to wear a different colour of attire:
and so my master speaks these words to me,
which you yourself shall hear without delay:

"This graceful and light-hearted youthful girl
is still a virgin; and the other one,
attired in mourning dress, is now a widow.
But since you can't love both at the same time,
it's only right that one should be our love:
so tell me soon which most appeals to you."

Concerning this I find I can't decide:
So I now turn to you. Which should I choose?

80b Reply by Antonio Pucci

You've come so forcefully into my heart
with your sweet unpretentious poetry
that day by day I find that all I wish
to do is serve you well and nothing else.
Although in all ways I rate less than you,
from what I know, I'd tell you to "Aim high,"
since with this kind of pointer Love will say
"Just pick the one that seems the best to you."

And if before he lets his arrow fly
he lets you choose what pleases you, accept
his help and do your best to honour him.
Whoever takes a virgin as his love
must study her expressions with mistrust,
for rarely what is promised is attained.

And so, as son to father, I'd urge you
to put aside the lily for the widow.

81a Riccio barbiere a messer Giovanni Boccaccio

S'io avesse più lingue che Carmente
non ebbe, o fosse Appollo in me inchiuso,
sarebbe el sole nell'Orïon rinchiuso
più d'una volta, del nostro orïente,
che io potesse dire enteramente
vostra magnificenza e moderno uso:
ond'io però di ciò a voi mi scuso
a guisa ch'al maestro fa el discente.

Ma più del dubbio ha presso lo 'ntelletto,
il qual di vera luce più m'affosca
che non fà<ce> la nebbia verde lama.
Se uom può più amar che non conosca
e s'e' conoscer può più che non ama,

come da voi per altra volta è detto,
da voi siami chiarito con effetto.

81b Risposta di Giovanni Boccaccio

Allor che 'l regno d'Etïopia sente
il rodopeo cristallo esser deluso,
e de' sui ogni serpe leva el muso,
surge a' mortali un nobile ascendente,
del qual fé la Sidonïa dolente
pruove, al parlar, che sai, alto e diffuso;
non Pompeo Magno, Giuba o il nobil Druso
videro el ciel oprare altrimente.

Però, se ben ti recherai al petto,
con quale ago vedrai punga la mosca
di ciò che 'l tuo disio sì caldo brama.
Vedrai ancora che la gente tósca
risponder sappia quand'altri la chiama,

e per ramogna rendere un sonetto:
ben ch'arte non sia a te qual l'intelletto.

81a Riccio the barber to Messer Giovanni Boccaccio

If I spoke better than Carmenta did,
or if Apollo were inside of me,
the sun would find itself in Orion
more than just one time in our orient
before I could speak thoroughly about
your great magnificence and modern style:
so I ask you to pardon me for this
the way a student would his lecturer.

But my mind gathers in itself more doubt,
which makes the light of truth obscure to me
more than the fog obscures a fertile plain.
Can he love better one he doesn't know,
and better know someone he does not love,

as has been said another time by you,
elucidate for to me with certainty.

81b Reply by Giovanni Boccaccio

When the realm of Ethiopia
can feel the ice high in the Rhodopes
has thawed and all its snakes lift up their heads,
a noble essence rises to us mortals
that made Queen Dido suffer many trials,
as is, you know, reported far and wide;
not Pompey the Great, Juba, nor good Drusus
observed the heavens moving differently.

And so if you give it sufficient thought,
you'll see how I present an argument
to answer what you keenly want to know.
You'll see too people here in Tuscany
know how to answer what is asked of them

and how to write a sonnet of good wishes,
although your talent's weaker than your wit.

82a Sonetto di ser Cecco di Meletto de' Rossi da Forlì mandato a messer Francesco Petrarca, a messer Lancillotto Anguissola, a maestro Antonio da Ferrara e a messer Giovanni Boccaccio

Voglia il ciel, voglia pur seguir l'editto
che imposto fu da prima alli ampi giri,
e rôte intorno l'orbe con quei spiri
che giungon li elementi e 'l centro inscritto!
ch'è per servar quello antico rescritto,
o che l'armata man ver' noi s'adiri
di Giove fulminando, o qual s'ammiri
di tenebre lunare el sol trafitto.

Non è alcun che si cuopra alle saette
avvelenate che 'l bel viver fura,
sì che l'uman valor fra i bruti mette;
e radi son che con la mente pura
conosca il suo Fattore o sue vendette:
ma Lui non val parlar con lingua scura.

Le stelle erranti osservan lor vïaggio,
né noi costringe a seguitar suo raggio.

82b Risposta del Petrarca

Perché l'eterno moto sopraditto
ciascun pianeto in sé rapido tiri,
divis'in parte per li moti giri,
sì come scrive il gran dottor d'Egitto;
né per combustïon d'alcun, che vitto
sia dai raggi delli accesi ardiri
di Febo, che sostenne li martirî
da sua sorella opposta al corso dritto:

nessun sarà, se Iddio non gliel permette,
che attento e fiso guardi la figura
del cielo adorno delle luci elette;
nel qual si può notar quanto sicura
e ferma nostra vita star s'aspette
nel fragil mondo opposto a sua natura.

Se l'intelletto umano è prode e saggio,
corso di stella non può farli oltraggio.

82a Sonnet by Ser Cecco of Meletto de' Rossi of Forlì sent to Messer Francesco Petrarca, Messer Lancillotto Anguissola, Maestro Antonio da Ferrara, and Messer Giovanni Boccaccio

Let heaven, even heaven, heed the law
that was at first imposed on the vast wheels,
and let the globe revolve with all the traits
that unify the elements and Earth!
which must observe the ancient principle,
that either the armed hand of Jove should hurl
his shafts towards us in anger or the sun
become transfixed with lunar cloudiness.

There's no one who can shield himself against
the poisoned shafts that steal away fair life,
so with the beasts it places human worth;
and there are few who understand their Maker
or his revenge with clarity of mind:
but He is not required to offer signs.

The moving stars keep to their orbit paths,
and they don't force us to obey their rays.

82b Reply by Petrarch

Since the eternal motion spoken of,
which is allotted to each moving wheel,
turns every planet quickly round itself,
as the great theorist of Egypt writes;
and insofar as any planet's burned,
because it's made a victim of the rays
of Phoebus's bright zeal, who suffered from
his sister's motion counter to his course,

no one, unless God offers his consent,
who keenly and intently gazes on
the sky adorned with all its noble lights,
is able to denote how much our life
can be expected to be safe and firm
in this frail world so hostile to its kind.

So, if the human mind is brave and wise,
the path a star takes cannot do it harm.

82c Risposta di messer Lancillotto Anguissola

Alzi lo 'ngegno ogn'uom con quello amitto
che aver conviensi ai valorosi viri,
e l'un pianeto né l'altro martiri
o nòi natura in quanto ha Dio prescritto.
El ciel sue leggi osservi circumscritto:
non si dimostri tal che l'uom sospiri,
non forse oltra il certo ordin circumspiri
l'ira di Dio, come fé già in Egitto.

L'umane gregge dal temer costrette,
non però di veder mente matura,
dal vizio con ragion tornan corrette,
però ch' e' par sol di virtù misura.
Ma contra coscïenza si commette
e, riposato il ciel, se n' va paura.

Così per entro uno scuro ed un raggio
ci porta arbitrio a pace ed a dannaggio.

82d Risposta di maestro Antonio da Ferrara

El cielo, e 'l firmamento suo, sta dritto
e guarda le sue rote ché nol tiri
fora d'i corsi naturali e viri,
per osservar quel che de lui è ditto.
Se 'l movimento suo fusse raffitto,
la luna, el sol ed altri suoi zaffiri,
dov'e' conven che l'universo miri,
darebber passïone al mondo afflitto.

L'umane genti son fatte sì strette
che de virtù e cortesia non cura,
e poco attende quel ch'egli 'mpromette.
Offende al suo Fattor e sua figura,
con gli altri bruti, del mal ch'e' commette:
però l'eterna pena lor matura.

Le stelle son de sì alto legnaggio
che nostra colpa li fa far omaggio.

82c Reply by Messer Lancillotto Anguissola

Let every man who wears attire required
of men of valour lift his intellect
and not give any planet agony,
or trouble nature for what God's ordained.
Let heaven carry out its tasks by law:
let it not operate as man would wish,
unless the wrath of God should go against
established norms, as He did once in Egypt.

The human herd constrained by fearfulness,
instead of thinking in a thoughtful way,
corrects its vices using reason's sway,
so that it seems but virtue's consequence.
But this is done against the force of conscience,
and so, once heaven's calm, their fears abate.

Therefore, by means of darkness and of light
free will leads us towards peace or injury.

82d Reply by Maestro Antonio da Ferrara

Heaven, and its firmament, is fixed
and sees that its rotations won't pull it
from its true natural trajectory,
to reaffirm what has been said of it.
This movement, if it were to terminate,
the moon, the sun and all its jewels as well,
where it befits it watch the universe,
would foist torment upon the world it rules.

Human beings are so unprincipled
that they give grace and virtue little thought
and barely carry through with what they vow.
They offend their Maker and his image,
as do wild beasts, through harm that they commit:
that's why they're punished by eternal pain.

The stars are of such lofty lineage
that our defects make us bow down to them.

82e Risposta di messer Giovanni Boccaccio

L'antiquo padre il cui primo delitto
ne fu cagion di morte e di sospiri
pose assai poco modo ai suoi desiri,
essendo stato pur allor descritto.
Ma quel ritroso popul, che d'Egitto
non senza affanno uscì dopo i martirî,
bench'ei vedessi mille fatti miri,
rade volte seguì consiglio dritto.

Per che <non> nòi se delle cose elette
più lontan siamo: seguitar misura
del ciel men grava all'anime perfette.
E benché spesso semplice paura
solare eclisse o squarciar nuvolette
faccia, chi 'l sente poco se ne cura.

Quel che morì per trarne di servaggio
mercé n'avrà per lo cammin selvaggio.

82f Replica di ser Cecco di Meletto a messer Giovanni Boccaccio

Quando redire al nido fu disditto
a Giulio Cesar, perché fûr deliri
gli padri col Senato e gli altri siri,
volse prima mostrar l'amar conflitto
el ciel perfidïoso, stando pitto
di fiamme rogge e d'ardenti papiri
di terribil' comete, e i color' niri
alla solar quadriga porse amitto.

Similemente fé sua luce bura
anzi che Bruto l'arme avesse strette
contra il sangue cesareo; e l'ampie mura
tuttor cascar si vede, con le vette
dell'alte torri sparse alla pianura,
per terremoti o vive folgorette.

Dunque ha ben pien di furia suo coraggio
chi non paventa natural dannaggio.

82e Reply by Messer Giovanni Boccaccio

The ancient father whose initial crime
became the origin of death and suffering
did very little to curb his desires,
despite his having been created then.
But that rebellious people, setting out
with toil from Egypt after their ordeals,
although they saw a thousand miracles,
would rarely follow counsel that was right.

So, we're not troubled being further from
divinity: to follow heaven's laws
is much less burdensome for perfect souls.
And while eclipses of the sun, or clouds
being ruptured, are cause for a little fear,
whoever feels it does not mind it much.

The one who died to end our servitude
will show us mercy on our trying journey.

82f Reply by Ser Cecco di Meletto to Messer Giovanni Boccaccio

When Julius Caesar was prevented from
returning home because the senators
and other lords behaved like lunatics,
an unpropitious heaven presaged first
the bitter conflict, making a display
of flames of crimson red and burning wicks
of terrifying comets, and a veil
of black obscured the solar chariot.

Its light was in the same way darkened just
before the moment Brutus drew his knife
against the blood of Caesar; everyday
we see immense walls fall, with pinnacles
of lofty towers strewn across the plain,
because of earthquakes or of lightning bolts.

So one must be completely arrogant
if one is unafraid of nature's scourge.

83a Annibale a Scipione

"I ciel', gl'iddii, l'età e la Fortuna,
secondo ai tuoi disiri, Iscipïone,
ti tiran forse fuor d'ogni ragione
a non voler con noi concordia alcuna.
Ma, se le mie vittorie ad una ad una
narrassi e la presente condizione,
forse porresti giù l'oppenïone
che splendida ti mostra la via bruna.

E vorresti più tosto certa pace
che speranza seguir talor fallace".

83b Risposta di Scipione ad Annibale

"Anibale, le paci che rompesti
dislëalmente a Sagunto mi fanno
certo che per punire il tüo inganno
arò gl'iddii alla mia gloria presti.
E come allora pace non volesti,
ancora a Roma servir ti faranno:
così acquistan color che non sanno
ne' lor tempi felici esser modesti.

Com'ïo t'ho qui d'Italia tirato,
così penso por fine al tüo stato".

83a Hannibal to Scipio

"The heavens and the gods, the age and Fortune,
propitious to your wishes, Scipio,
perhaps deprive you of all reason for
not wanting to agree with us at all.
But if I were to narrate one by one
my victories and cite my present state,
perhaps you might abandon your set view
that the dark way seems wonderful to you.

Then you would rather want a certain peace
than cleave to any hope that might be false."

83b Scipio's Reply to Hannibal

"Hannibal, the peace accords you broke
disloyally at Sagunto make me
most certain that to punish your deceit
I'll have the gods be ready for my fame.
And since you did not want peace at that time,
they'll once again make you a slave to Rome:
such is the gain for those who do not know
how to be moderate when times are good.

Since I have drawn you here from Italy,
I will have put an end to your regime."

84

Quante fïate per ventura il loco
vegg'io là dov'io fui da Amore preso,
tanto mi par di nuovo esser acceso
da un desio più caldo assai che 'l foco;
e poi che quello ho riguardato un poco
e stato alquanto sovra me sospeso,
dico: "Se tu ti fosse qui difeso,
non sarest'or, per merzé chieder, fioco.

Adunque piangi, poi la libertate
avevi nelle man' lasciat' hai andare
per donna vaga e di poca pietate".
Poi mi rivolgo, e dico che lo stare
subbietto a sì mirabile biltate
è somma e lieta libertate usare.

85

"A quella parte ov'io fui prima accesa
del piacer di colui che mai del core
non mi si partirà sovente Amore
mi tira, né mi vale il far difesa.
Quindi rimiro lui, tutta sospesa,
in giù e 'n su, pregandol, se 'l valore
suo sempre cresca, che 'l vago splendore
mi mostri del mio ben, che m'ha sì presa.

Il qual s'avvien che io veggia per grazia,
contenta dentro mi ritraggo un poco,
lodando Iddio, Amore e la Fortuna.
E mentre che d'averlo visto sazia
esser mi credo, raccender il foco
sento di rivederlo, e torno in una".

84

As many times as I pass by the place
where I was captured by the lord of Love,
so many do I seem aroused again
by a desire that's far more hot than fire;
and since I've given this a little thought
and having lingered over it somewhat,
I say: "If you'd defended yourself here,
you'd not now be, from asking pity, hoarse.

So, weep, since you have let the liberty
you had within your hands just slip away
for an unfaithful woman of scant pity."
And then I think again and say: to be
subjected to such wondrous loveliness
is to have a great pleasing liberty.

85

"Love draws me to the place where I was first
enraptured by the beauty of the one
who never will be parted from my heart,
and I'm unable to defend myself.
And so, held fast, I gaze at him from top
to bottom, begging him, may his worth grow
continually, that he display to me
the splendour of my love, which seized me so.

Should I see him by grace, I'll happily
draw back within myself a little bit,
commending God, and Love, and Fortune too.
And while I think that I am satisfied
to have seen him, in seeing him I feel
the fire revive, and I look back at him."

86

S'io ti vedessi, Amor, pur una volta
l'arco tirar e saettar costei,
forse ch'alcuna speme prenderei
di pace, ancor, della mia pena molta;
ma perché baldanzosa, lieta e sciolta
la veggio e te codardo inver' di lei,
non so ben da qual parte i dolor' miei
s'aspettin fine, o l'anima ricolta.

Ogni suo atto impenna un de' tuo strali;
che diss'io un? ma cento: e il tuo arco
ognor a trapassar mi par più forte.
Vedi ch'io son senz'armi, diseguali
al poter tuo! E se non chiudi il varco,
l'anima mia, ch'è tua, se n' vol'a morte.

87

Trovato m'hai, Amor, solo e senz'armi,
là dove più armato ed avveduto
sei, credo, per uccidermi venuto
col favor di costei, ch'in disertarmi
aguzza le saette che passarmi
deöno il cor. Ma, poi ch'e' fia saputo,
certo son ne sarai da men tenuto
d'aver voluto pur così disfarmi.

Poco onor ti sarà, s'io non m'inganno,
ferir, vincer, legar, uccider uno
che far non puote inver' di te difesa.
Ma tu, che ad onor rispetto alcuno
non avesti giammai, del mio gran danno
ti riderai: e io m'avrò l'offesa.

86

Were I, lord Love, to see you even once
discharge an arrow that pierced into her,
perhaps I'd take a little bit of hope
that my deep pain might one day find relief;
but since I see that she is daring, free
and happy, and that you are cowardly
towards her, I do not know how to expect
my pain to end, or my soul to be saved.

Each act of hers lets loose one of your darts;
did I say one? a hundred: and your bow
continually appears to gain more strength.
You see that I'm unarmed, and cannot match
your might! And if you do not close my wound,
my soul, which is yours too, will fly to death.

87

You've found me, Love, defenseless and alone,
whereas you, being more astute and armed,
have come, I think, to slay me on behalf of her,
who, wishing to destroy me utterly,
now sharpens arrows that are meant to pass
right through my heart. But after this is known,
I'm certain that you will be less admired
for having sought to kill me in this way.

You'll gain no honour, if I'm not deceived,
to wound, defeat, tie up, and execute
one who cannot defend himself from you.
But you, who's never had respect at all
for honour, will just mock my injury:
and I will suffer this indignity.

88

"Che fabrichi? che tenti? ché limando
vai le catene in che tu stesso entrasti
– mi dice Amore – e te stesso legasti
senza mio prego e senza mio comando?
Che latebra, che fuga vai cercando
di drieto a me, al qual tu obligasti
la fede tua, allor che tu mirasti
l'angelica bellezza desïando?

O stolte menti, o animali sciocchi!
poi che t'avrai co' tua inganni sciolto
e volando sarai fuggito via,
una parola, un riso, un muover d'occhi,
un dimonstrarsi lieto il vago volto
farà tornarti più stretto che pria".

89

Se Zefiro omai non disacerba
il cor aspro e feroce di costei,
più mai non spero, per gridar omei,
trovar riposo a la mia pena acerba.
Ma sì com'el rinnova i fiori e l'erba
e piante state morte mesi sei,
così porria far dolc'e verde lei,
pietosa in vista, in fatti men superba.

Questa speranza sola ancor mi resta,
per la qual vivo, ingagliardisco e tremo
dubbiando che la Morte non me invole.
Ond'io, prima che venga al punto estremo,
Fortuna prego non mi sia molesta
cotanto ai piacer' miei quanto la suole.

88

“What are you doing, trying to do, by filing
the chains which you got into willingly”
– Love tells me – “and in which you bound yourself
without my asking and with no command?
What hideaway, what haven do you seek
behind my back, you having promised me
your fealty, when you had looked at her
angelic loveliness with deep desire?

O senseless minds, O foolish human beings!
When your enchantment will have been dispelled
and you will have since taken flight and fled,
a word, a smile, a movement of the eyes,
a joyful display of her lovely face
will make you cling more tightly than before.”

89

If Zephyr has by now not pacified
her cruel and savage heart, I find that I
can never hope again, however much
I cry, to gain relief from my raw pain.
But just as he renews the flowers, the grass
and plants that have lain lifeless for six months,
so too could he make her look sweet, alive
and merciful, less proud in bearing too.

This is the only hope that I have left,
for which I live, keep myself strong and shake
with fear that Death will carry me away.
And so, before I reach the final pass,
I ask that Fortune be not harsh with me
as much as it is with my happiness.

90

L'alta speranza che li mia martirî
soleva mitigare alcuna volta,
in noiosa fortuna ora rivolta,
de' dolci mia pensier' fatt'ha sospiri.
E gli amorosi e caldi mia desiri,
lacrime divenuti, la raccolta
rabbia per gli occhi fuor dal cor disciolta
<spargon in mille rivi con sospiri>.

Oh, s'io potesse creder di vedere
canuta e crespa e pallida colei
che con isdegno nuovo n'è cagione!
Ch'ancor la vita mia di ritenere,
che fugge, a più poter m'ingegnerei,
per rider la cambiata condizione.

91

S'egli avvien mai che tanto gli anni miei
lunghi si faccin che le chiome d'oro
vegga d'argento, ond'io or m'innamoro,
e crespo farsi il viso di costei,
e cispi gli occhi bei, che tanto rei
son per me, lasso!, ed il caro tesoro
del sen ritrarsi, e il suo canto sonoro
divenir roco, sì com'io vorrei:

ogni mio spirto, ogni dolore e pianto
si farà riso; e pur sarò sì pronto
ch'io dirò: "Donna, Amor non t'ha più cara;
più non adesca il tuo söave canto;
pallid'e vizza non sei più in conto:
ma pianger pòi l'essere stata avara".

90

The high hope that once used to mitigate
my sufferings at times, now having changed
into an aggravating discontent,
has caused my sweet thoughts to become deep sighs.
And my enraptured and intense desires,
turned into tears, the harvest of my wrath
released outside my heart through my sad eyes,
<disperse into a thousand streams with sighs>.

Oh, if I ever thought I might see her
with white and wavy hair and pallid face,
she who's the cause of my unique disdain!
As much as I am able to, I'd find
a way to carry on my life, which ebbs,
to laugh about the change in her appearance.

91

If it should ever happen that my years
are so drawn out I see her golden hair,
which makes me love her now, turn silvery,
and see her worn out face with wrinkled lines,
her lovely eyes form crust, which are for me,
alas!, so wicked, and her cherished breast
begin to sag, and her sonorous voice
grow raspy, just as I would want it to,

my spirits, pains, and cries, each one will turn
to laughter; and, too, I'll be quick to say:
"My lady, Love no longer holds you dear;
no longer will your silken voice beguile;
turned pale and withered, you no longer count:
but you can mourn your former stinginess."

92

Quante fïate indrieto mi rimiro
e vegg'io l'ore e i giorni e i mesi e gli anni
ch'io ho perduto seguendo gl'inganni
della folle speranza e del desiro,
vegg'io il pericol corso e il martiro
sofferto invan in gli amorosi affanni,
né trovar credo chi di ciò mi sganni,
tanto ne piango e contro a me m'adiro.

E maledico il dì che prima vidi
gli occhi spietati che Amor guidaro
pe' miei nel cor, che lasso e vinto giace.
O crudel Morte, perché non m'uccidi?
Tu sola puoi il mio dolor amaro
finire e pormi, forse, in lieta pace.

93

"L'arco degli anni tuoi trapassat'hai,
cambiato il pelo e la virtù mancata;
di questa tüo picciola giornata
già verso 'l vespro camminando vai:
buono è adunque Amor lasciare omai,
ed a pensar dell'ultima posata"
dice l'anima seco, innamorata,
qualor punta è da non usati guai.

Ma come l'ombra vede di colei
– non vo' dir gli occhi – che nel mondo venne
per dar sempre cagione a' sospir' miei,
così all'alto vol si trae le penne,
e ' passi volge tutti a seguir lei,
come fé già quando me' si convenne.

92

As often as I reminisce about
and count the hours and days and months and years
that I have lost as victim of deceit,
which fostered foolish hope and mad desire,
I see the danger risked and suffering
endured in vain in amorous distress,
and I doubt anyone would question this,
so much I weep and fume against myself.

And so I curse the day that I first saw
her ruthless eyes, which steered Love through my own
into my heart, that lies now tired and ruined.
O cruel Death, why don't you take my life?
For you alone can end my bitter pain
and bring me to, perhaps, a joyful peace.

93

"You have surpassed the high point of your years,
and with your hair turned grey and strength now gone,
you are progressing towards the eventide
of this short day that has been granted you:
the time is right for you to cast off Love
and give thought to your final resting place,"
my soul says to itself, still much in love,
whenever stung by unfamiliar grief.

But when it sees the shadow of the one
– and not to say her eyes – who came into
this world to give rise to my constant sighs,
then to the lofty flight it rests its wings
and turns and wends its way to follow her,
as it did when it was more opportune.

94

S'io veggio il giorno, Amor, che mi scapestri
de' lacci tua, che sì mi stringon forte,
vaga bellezza né parole accorte
né alcun' altri mai piacer' terrestri
tanto potranno, ch'io più m'incapestri
o mi rimetta nelle tua ritorte:
avanti andrò, fin che venga la Morte,
pascendo l'erbe per gli luoghi alpestri.

Tu m'haï il cibo, il sonno ed il riposo
ed il parer uom fra gli altri ed il pensiero
tolto che io di me aver devrei,
e hâmi fatto del vulgo noioso
favola divenire: ond'io dispero
mai poter ritrovar quel ch'io vorrei.

95

Quand'io riguardo me, vie più che 'l vetro
fragile, e gli anni fuggir com'il vento,
sì pietoso di me meco divento
che dir nol porria lingua non che metro,
piangendo il tempo c'ho lasciat'arietro
mal operato, e prendendo spavento
de' casi, i quai talora a cento a cento
posson del viver tôrmi il cammin tetro.

Né mi può doglia, per ciò, né paura
la vaga donna trarmi della mente,
dov'Amor disegnò la sua figura.
Per che, s'io non m'inganno, certamente
la fine a quest'amor la sepultura
darà, ed altro no, ultimamente.

94

If I, Love, see the day when you release
me from your bonds, which bind me stringently,
her lovely beauty and her prudent words
and any other pleasure in the world
will never be enough to make me bind
or fasten myself in your ropes again:
I'll rather keep on, till Death comes for me,
consuming grass up in the alpine peaks.

You've taken from me food and sleep and rest
and looking like a man as others can
and thinking of myself as I ought to,
and made of me a laughing stock before
the tiresome crowd: so I despair of ever
getting back what I would want to have.

95

When I look at myself, by far more fragile
than glass, and see the years flee like the wind,
then I become so piteous of myself
that I cannot speak let alone write verse,
lamenting all the time I've left behind
so poorly spent, and growing fearful of
events, which sometimes by the hundreds can
remove me from the bleak road of my life.

So, therefore, neither pain nor fearfulness
can take that lovely lady from my mind,
where Love inscribed the image of her form.
And if I'm not mistaken, certainly
my burial, and nothing else, will end
the love I bear her, with finality.

96

S'Amor, li cui costumi già molt'anni
con sospir' infiniti provat'hai,
t'è or più grave che l'usato assai,
perché, seguendol, te medesmo inganni
credendo trovar pace tra gli affanni?
perché da lui non ti scavresti omai?
perché nol fuggi? E forse ancor avrai,
libero, alcun riposo de' tua danni.

Non si racquista il tempo che si perde
per perder tempo, né mai lagrimare
per lagrimar restette, com'uom vede.
Bastiti ch'ad Amor il tempo verde,
misero!, desti. Ed ora, ch'a imbiancare
cominci, di te stesso abbia mercede!

97

"Era 'l tuo ingegno divenuto tardo
e la memoria confusa e smarrita
e l'anima gentil quasi 'nvilita
driet'al riposo del mondo bugiardo,
quando t'accese 'l mio vago riguardo
e suscitò la virtù tramortita,
tanto ch'io t'ho condotto ove s'invita
al gloriöso fin ciascun gagliardo.

In te sta el venir, se l'intelletto
aguzzi, driet'a me, che la corona
ti serbo delle frondi tanto amate.
Che farai? Vienne!" mi dice nel petto
la donna per la quale Amor mi sprona.
Ed io mi sto: tant'è la mia viltate!

96

If Love, whose conduct you for many years
have suffered through with infinite deep sighs,
is now more painful than it used to be,
why, clinging to it, do you cheat yourself
by thinking you'll find peace beside your woes?
Why don't you free yourself from him right now?
Why don't you flee? And then perhaps you might,
being free, find rest from all your injuries.

You can't reclaim the time that you have lost
by losing still more time, nor ever weep
to end your weeping, as is quite well known.
Let it suffice you gave your youthful years,
forlorn!, to Love. And now that you begin
to turn all white, take mercy on yourself!

97

"Your quick and clever wit had lost its strength,
your memory now grown confused and frail,
your noble soul corrupted more or less,
bound by the comfort of the lying crowd,
when my attractive glance aroused in you
and brought to life your virtue that lay stunned,
so much so that I've led you to the place
where all brave men are stirred to win high praise.

It's left to you, if you should put your mind
to it, to follow me, for I reserve
for you the crown of leaves that you so love.
What will you do? Come now!" my lady says
within my heart for whom Love spurs me on.
Yet I hold back: such is my cowardice!

98

Parmi tal volta, riguardando il sole,
vederl'assai più che l'usato acceso:
per ch'io con meco dico: "Forse esteso
si siede in quello il mio fervente sole,
il quale agli occhi miei sempre fu sole
poscia ch'io fui ne' lacci d'Amor preso.
Per certo ei v'è: però di tanto peso
son ora e raggi di quest'altro sole".

E sì nel cor s'impronta esto pensero
ch'e' mi pare veder, guardando in esso,
sì come aquila fàce, intento e fiso,
la *fiamma* mia, e d'essa assai intero
ogni contegno, e conoscer da presso
li capei d'oro e crespi ed il bel viso.

99

Dormendo un giorno, in sonno mi parea
quasi pennuto volar verso il cielo
drieto all'orme di quella il cui bel velo
cenere è fatto, ed ella è fatta dea.
Quivi sì vaga e lieta la vedea
ch'arder mi parve di più caldo gelo
ch'io non solea, e dileguarsi il gelo
ch'in pianto doloroso mi tenea.

E guardando, l'angelica figura
la man distese, come se volesse
prender la mia; ed io mi risvegliai.
Oh quanta fu la mia disavventura!
Chi sa, se ella allor preso m'avesse,
se io quaggiù più ritornava mai?

98

From time to time as I look at the sun
it seems much brighter than is usual.
And so I ask myself: "Perhaps a place
inside of it contains my burning sun,
which to my eyes has always been the sun
since I was captured in the snares of Love.
It surely must be there: that's why the rays
are now so potent from this other sun."

So clearly in my heart this thought imprints
itself, that looking at it, I appear to see,
just like an eagle with its gaze intent,
my *flame*, and all the attributes she has,
entirely, and recognize up close
her golden curly locks and lovely face.

99

Asleep one day, within a dream I seemed
to see myself fly heavenward on wings
behind the wake of her whose lovely shape
has turned to dust, and she into a goddess.
I saw her here so lovely and so kind
that I thought I burned in a hotter ice
than I had known before, and all the ice
that held me in sad tears then melt away.

As I was watching, her angelic form
put out its hand, extending it as if
she wished to take my own; then I awoke.
Alas, how great was my adversity!
Who knows, perhaps if she had taken it,
I never would have come back down again.

100

Se la *fiamma* degli occhi ch'or son santi
e che per me fûr dardi e poi catene,
mortificasse alquanto le mia pene
e rasciugasse e grevi e lunghi pianti,
io udirei quelli angelici canti
ch'ode chi vede il sommo e vero Bene,
né vagando anderei drieto alla spene
ch'in questa vita molti ne fa erranti.

Ma essa, eterna, le cose mortali
disdegna, e ride del pensier fallace
che mi sospinge dov'ognor più ardo;
per che temo che mai alle mia ali
non verran penne che a tanta pace
levar mi possan dal mondo bugiardo.

101

"Che cerchi, stolto? che dintorno miri?
Cenere sparta son le membra in ch'io
piacqui già tanto al tuo caldo desio
e mossi il petto ai pietosi desiri.
Perché non lièvi gli occhi agli alti giri?
Io dico al ciel, anz'al regno di Dio,
dove più bel che mai il viso mio
veder potrai, e pien de' tuoi desiri".

Così con meco talora ragiona
la bella donna, vedendo cercarmi
quel che giammai quaggiù veder non deggio.
Ma, come, ravveduto, m'abbandona,
piangendo penso come qui impennarmi
possa e volar al suo beato seggio.

100

If the *flame* of her eyes, now sanctified,
which were for me first arrows and then chains,
was to alleviate my pain somewhat
and dry my heavy and protracted tears,
I'd hear the melodies the angels sing,
which one who sees the highest Good can hear,
and not go straying after vain desires
that cause so many in this life to err.

But she, who is eternal, now disdains
all mortal things and mocks fallacious thoughts
that always drive me where I burn the most;
this makes me fear my wings will never have
such feathers as I need to rise above
the lying world to such a peace as hers.

101

"Still searching, fool? Still looking everywhere?
My body's members are now scattered ash
by which I once pleased your intense desire
and drew forth sighs of pity from your breast.
Why don't you lift your eyes to see the spheres?
I mean high heaven, indeed the realm of God,
where you may see my face more beautiful
than ever, and all full of your desires."

This is the way my lovely lady speaks
with me at times while she observes me search
for what I never can see here below.
But, penitent, as she abandons me,
in tears I think how I might put on wings
and fly aloft up to her sacred seat.

102

Dante, se tu nell'amorosa spera,
com'io credo, dimori riguardando
la bella Bice, la qual già cantando
altra volta ti trasse là dov'era,
se per cambiar fallace vita a vera
amor non se n'oblia, io ti domando
per lei, di grazia, ciò che, contemplando,
a far ti fia assai cosa leggera.

Io so che, infra l'altre anime liete
del terzo ciel, la mia Fiammetta vede
l'affanno mio dopo la sua partita:
pregala, se 'l gustar dolce di Lete
non la m'ha tolta, in luogo di merzede
a sé m'impetri tosto la salita.

103

Era sereno il ciel, di stelle adorno,
e i venti tutti nelle lor caverne
posavono, e le nuvolette alterne
resolute eron tutte intorno intorno,
quand'una *fiamma* più chiara che 'l giorno,
rimirand'io alle cose superne,
veder mi parve per le strade eterne
volando fare al suo loco ritorno,

e di quella ver' me nascer parole,
le quai dicìen: "Chi meco esser desia
benign'esser convien ed ubidiente
e d'umiltà vestito; e s'altro vuole
cammin tener, giammai meco non fia
nel sacro regno della lieta gente".

102

Dante, if you dwell in the sphere of love,
as I believe you do, beholding her,
the lovely Bice, who already once
before, while singing, brought you where she was,
if one does not forget the force of love
in changing from the false life to the true,
I ask you, please, on her behalf, to do,
by thinking, something that's not difficult.

I know among the other happy souls
of the third sphere my Fiammetta sees
the anguish I've felt after her departure:
beseech her, if the sweet taste of Lethe
has not made her forget me, rather than
show pity, to have me soon brought to her.

103

The sky was clear and calm, adorned with stars,
and every breeze of air lay peacefully
within its cave, and all the clouds outside
had fully disappeared from every part,
when brighter than the day, I seemed to see,
as I was looking at supernal things,
a *flame* along the pathways of the heavens
in flight returning to its residence,

and from it words then issue forth to me,
which said: "He who desires to be with me
must be kindhearted and obedient
and clothed in humbleness; and should he seek
a different path, he'll never be with me
within the sacred realm of happy souls."

104

Le rime, le quai già fece sonore
la voce giovinil ne' vaghi orecchi
e che movien de' mia pensier' parecchi
a quel desio che m'infiammava il core
scrivendole com <l>e dettava Amore,
han fatto chiocce gli anni gravi e vecchi,
poscia che Morte ruppe quelli specchi
da' quai forza prendea lo mio vigore.

E come 'l viso angelico tornossi
al regno là dond'era a noi venuto
per farne fede dell'altrui bellezza
e i passi miei di drieto a lui fûr mossi,
né rima poi né verso m'è piaciuto,
né altro che 'l seguir la sua altezza.

105

D'Omero non poté 'l celeste ingegno
a pien mostrar d'Elèna 'l vago riso,
né Zeusi, dopo, l'alt'e bel diviso,
quantunque avesse di molte il disegno:
e però contro a me stesso non sdegno
se 'l gloriöso ben di paradiso
scriver non so, né l'angelico viso
c'ha 'l mio cor seco nel celeste regno.

Ma chi desia veder quella bellezza
che, sola, tenne in la vita mortale
d'uom non aspetti alcun dimostramento,
ma di sacra virtù s'impenni l'ale
e sù se n' voli in la suprema altezza:
lì la vedrà, e rimarrà contento.

104

The lyrics that my youthful voice once made
so resonant to sympathetic ears
and which sprang from my thoughts so similar
to that desire which set my heart on fire,
composing them as Love dictated them,
have made the burdensome and late years harsh,
ever since cruel Death destroyed those eyes,
from which my fortitude derived its strength.

And after her angelic face had gone
back to the realm from which she'd come to us
to give proof of another's loveliness
and after I'd begun to follow it,
no lyric, not one verse, has pleased me since,
but only to pursue her loveliness.

105

Homer's divine creativity
could not portray in full Helen's fair smile,
nor, later, Zeuxis her fair noble form,
though for his portrait he used many models:
so, therefore, I do not disdain myself
if I cannot describe the glorious good
of paradise, nor the angelic face
that holds my heart in the celestial realm.

But one desiring to see beauty such
as this which she alone had in this world
should not expect to see a work of art,
but rather put on wings of sacred power
and fly above up to the highest heaven:
there he will see her, and will be content.

106

Sì acces'e fervente è il mio desio
di seguitar colei che quivi in Terra
con il suo altero sdegno mi fé guerra
infin allor ch'al ciel se ne salìo
che, non ch'altri, ma me metto in oblio.
E parmi nel pensier, che sovent'erra,
quella gravezza perder che m'atterra
e quasi uccel levarmi verso Dio:

e trapassar le spere e pervenire
davanti al divin trono, infra i beati,
e lei veder, che seguirla mi fàce,
sì bella ch'io non so poscia ridire,
quando ne' luoghi lor son ritornati
gli spiriti, che van cercando pace.

107

O Giustizia regina, al mondo freno,
mossa d'alta Virtù dal sommo cielo,
or fredda e pigra sta' coverta a velo!
Rompe quest'aire e mostra tutt'el corso,
e scendi con tuo forze e con l'ardire,
ché tal virtù non manchi al buon disire.

Fenda l'usata spada, e non con fretta,
che ' colpi non fien tardi a chi gli aspetta.

106

So strong and so intense is my desire
to follow her, who here on Earth made war
against me with her arrogant disdain
up to the moment she rose heavenward,
that I forget myself, not only others.
And in my thought, part fantasy, I seem
to lose the weight that holds me down to earth
and rise above towards God just like a bird,

to pass beyond the spheres and come before
the sacred throne among the blessed ones,
and see the one who makes me climb to her,
whose beauty is so great it can't be told,
when my spirits, which only seek for peace,
have come back to the place where they belong.

107

O Justice, queen who keeps the world in check,
moved by the highest heaven's lofty power,
now cold and tired, you're covered by a veil!
May the sky burst and show the path you take,
may you descend with strength and bravery,
so that your power fulfills your good intent.

Employ your well-worn sword, yet not with haste,
so timely blows strike those who merit them.

108

Fuggit'è ogni virtù, spent'è il valore
che fece Italia già donna del mondo,
e le Muse castalie son in fondo,
né cura quas'alcun del lor onore.
Del verde lauro più fronda né fiore
in pregio sono, e ciascun sotto il pondo
dell'arricchir sottentra, e del profondo
surgono i vizi trïonfando fore.

Per che, se i maggior' nostri hanno lasciato
il vago stil de' versi e delle prose,
esser non dèti maraviglia alcuna.
Piangi dunque con meco il nostro stato,
l'uso moderno e l'opre vizïose,
cui oggi favoreggia la Fortuna.

109

Apizio lègge nelle nostre scole
e 'l re Sardanapalo, e lor dottrina
di gran lunga è preposta alla divina
dagli ozî disonesti e dalle gole.
E verità né in fatti né in parole
oggi si truova, e ciaschedun inchina
all'Avarizia sì com'a reina,
la quale in tutto può ciò che la vuole.

Onestà s'è partita e Cortesia,
ed ogn'altra Virtù è al ciel tornata,
ed insieme con esse Leggiadria,
dalle villane menti discacciata.
Ma quanto questo per durar si sia
Iddio se l' sa, ch'ad ogni cosa guata.

108

All virtue's fled, what is of value dead,
which made Italia lady of the world,
and the Castalian Muses are suppressed
and almost no one cares to honour them.
The verdant laurel's foliage and flowers
are not esteemed, and everyone beneath
the spell of riches gains reward, and from
the bottom vices surge victorious.

Yet if our ancestors have cast aside
the pleasant style in poetry and prose,
you ought not in the slightest be surprised.
And so lament with me our common lot,
the modern ways and enterprise of vice,
which Fortune favours at the present time.

109

Apicius and Sardanapalus
the king are read in school, and their beliefs
are very much preferred to sacred thought
by evil idlers and by greedy men.
No truth is found today in word or deed,
and everyone bows down upon their knees
in front of Avarice, as to a queen
who can do anything that pleases her.

Integrity and Courtesy have fled,
and every other Virtue has returned
to heaven, and with them true Gracefulness,
rejected by uncultivated minds.
But just how long this circumstance will last
God knows, who keeps his eye on everything.

110

Saturno al coltivar la terra puose
già lungo studio, e Pallàde lo ingegno
alle meccaniche arti, ed Ercul degno
si fé di eterna fama l'orgogliose
fiere domando; e l'opre virtüose
de' buon' Romani el nome loro e 'l regno
ampliâr ultra ad ogni mortal segno,
e di Alessandro le imprese animose.

Così filosofia fece Platone,
Aristotele ed altri assai famosi,
ed Omero e Vergilio i versi loro.
Oggi serìa reputato un montone
chi torcesse el camin dalli studiosi
di perder tempo ad acquistar tesoro.

111

Tanto ciascun ad acquistar tesoro
con ogni ingegno s'è rivolto e dato
che quasi a dito per matto è mostrato
chi con virtù seguisce altro lavoro.
Per che constante stare infra costoro
oggi conviensi, nel mondo svïato,
a chi, come tu fosti, è infiammato,
Febo, del sacro e glorïoso alloro.

Ma perché tutto non può la virtute
ciò che la vuol, senza divino aiuto,
a te ricorro, e prego mi sostegni
contr'alli venti avversi a mia salute,
e, dopo il giusto affanno, il già canuto
capo d'alloro incoronar ti degni.

110

Long and hard did Saturn study ways
to cultivate the soil, as Pallas did
to aid the servile arts, and Hercules
made himself worthy of eternal fame
by taming brazen beasts; and daring feats
of noble Romans brought their citizens
and state renown beyond all mortal bounds,
as, too, did Alexander's valiant deeds.

And Plato likewise in philosophy,
and Aristotle, others of great fame,
as Homer and as Virgil did in verse.
Today we'd call a beast whoever turned
away from following the erudite
in wasting time at building up their wealth.

111

So much has everyone turned their sights to
and put their efforts on acquiring wealth
that one who does some other kind of work
with diligence is singled out as mad.
Therefore, these days whoever is inspired,
as you were, Phoebus, by the glorious
and sacred laurel wreath, must carry on
with life continuously among such ilk.

And yet since virtue cannot bring about
whatever it might wish without divine
support, I turn to you and pray you might
sustain my welfare against adverse winds,
and, after my just toil, you deign to place
upon my grey-haired head the laurel wreath.

112

Mentre sperai e l'uno e l'altro collo
transcender di Parnaso e ber dell'onde
del castalïo fonte e delle fronde
che già più ch'altre piacquero ad Apollo,
adornarmi le tempie, umìl rampollo
de' dicitori antichi, alle gioconde
rime mi diedi; e benché men profonde
fosser, cantâne in stil leggero e sollo.

Ma poscia che 'l cammino aspro e selvaggio
e gli anni miei già faticati e bianchi
tolser la speme del sù pervenire,
vinto, lasciai la speme del vïaggio,
le rime e i versi e i miei pensieri stanchi:
ond'or non so, com'io solea già, dire.

113

Il vivo fonte di Parnaso e quelle
frondi che furn'ad Appollo più care
m'ha fatto lungo tempo Amor cercare
driet'alla guida delle vaghe stelle
che, fra l'ombre salvatiche, le belle
Muse già fêr molte volte cantare;
né m'ha voluto Fortuna prestare
d'esser potuto pervenire ad elle.

Credo n'ha colpa il mio debil ingegno,
ch'alzar non può a vol sì alto l'ale
e non ha già studio o tempo perduto.
Darò dunche riposo all'alma frale,
e mi dorrò di non aver potuto
di quelle farmi, faticando, degno.

112

While hoping to cross over both the one
and other peak of Parnassus, and drink
from the Castalian spring, and ornament
my forehead with the fronds more pleasing to
Apollo than all others, I began
composing cheerful poems, as humble heir
of poets of the past; though less profound,
I sang them in a light and simple style.

But after harsh and savage journeying
and years of weariness in my old age
deprived me of my hope to reach my goal,
defeated, I gave up my journey's hope,
my poems, verses, and my tired thoughts:
I don't know what, as once I did, to write.

113

The living waters of Parnassus Spring
and fronds of which Apollo was most fond
that Love for many years made me seek out
beneath the guidance of the lovely stars
which the fair Muses, inside shaded groves,
made me sing frequently about before;
yet Fortune did not wish to tender me
the strength I needed to attain my goal.

I think the fault's the weakness of my wit,
for it can't lift its wings to fly so high
and it's not lost its passion or been slack.
I'll therefore give my feeble soul a rest,
and I'll regret not being capable
of proving myself worthy, though I've strived.

114

Dura cosa è ed orribile assai
la morte ad aspettare, e paürosa,
ma così certa ed infallibil cosa
né fu né è né, credo, sarà mai.
E 'l corso della vita è breve, c'hai,
e volger non si può né dargli posa;
né qui si vede cosa sì gioiosa
che 'l suo fine non sia lagrime e guai.

Dunque, perché con operar valore
non c'ingegniamo di stender la fama
e con quella far lunghi e brevi giorni?
Questa ne dà, questa ne serve onore,
questa ne lieva degli anni la squama,
questa ne fa di lunga vita adorni.

115

Assai sem raggirati in alto mare;
e quanto possan gli émpiti de' venti,
l'onde commosse e i fier' accidenti
provat'abbiamo. Né già il navicare
alcun segno, con vela o con vogare,
scampati ci ha dai perigli eminenti
fra ' duri scogli e le secche latenti,
ma sol Colui che ciò ch'e' vuol può fare.

Tempo è omai da reducersi in porto
e l'ancore fermare a quella pietra
che del Tempio congiunse e dua parieti;
quivi aspettar el fin del viver corto
nell'amor di Colui da cui s'impetra
con umiltà la vita de' quïeti.

114

Awaiting death is something difficult
and horrible, and also frightening,
but there has never been, nor is, I think,
nor will be, anything so sure and true.
The span of life is brief, the one you have,
and it cannot be turned around or paused;
we find here nothing that's so wonderful
that does not end in tears and suffering.

So why not use our ingenuity
to spread our fame about through worthy acts
and with that make our brief days become long?
This profits us, this safeguards our prestige,
this eases up the burden of our years,
this will adorn us with a life that's long.

115

So many times we've sailed out on the sea,
and of the blustering of perilous winds,
the mighty waves and violent incidents
we've had experience. And yet no sign
to guide us on our way, by sail or oar,
has ever saved us from the threats that loom
among the rocky cliffs or hidden shoals,
but He alone who does but what he wills.

It now is time to point the ship towards port
and put down anchor at the rock that joined
the two wall faces of the Temple's dome,
and here await the end of this short life
in loving Him, to whom we modestly
appeal to grant us the life of the blessed.

116

Quante fïate indrieto mi rimiro,
m'accorgo e veggio ch'io ho trapassato,
forse perduto e male adoperato,
seguendo in compiacermi alcun desiro,
tante con meco dolente m'adiro
sentendo quel ch'a tutti sol n'è dato
esser così fuggito, anzi cacciato
da me, che ora indarno ne sospiro.

<N>é so s'è conceduto che ' mia danni
ristorar possa ancor di bel soggiorno
in questa vita labile e meschina,
perché passato è l'arco de' mia anni,
e ritornar non posso al primo giorno:
e l'ultimo già veggio s'avicina.

117

Fuggesi il tempo, e 'l misero dolente
a cui si presta ad acquistar virtute,
fama perenne e eterna salute,
el danno irreparabile non sente;
ma neghittoso forma nella mente
cagion all'ozio e scusa alle perdute
doti, le quai poi, tardi conosciute,
piange, tapino, e senza pro si pente.

Surge col sol la piccola formica
nel tempo estivo, e si raguna l'ésca,
di che nel fredd'avverso si nutrica.
Al negligente sempr'e' par ch'incresca:
ond'e' nel verno muore od ei mendica,
e spesse volte senza lenza pésca.

116

As often as I look back on the past,
I come to understand the time I've spent,
perhaps being lost and not well occupied,
pursuing some desire to bring delight,
so often I grow angry with myself
for feeling what is given to us all
has hurried by, indeed which I have thrown
away, so now I grieve for it in vain.

I do not know if it is possible
to still redeem my losses with a place
that's better in this fragile, painful life;
because the high point of my years has passed,
and I cannot return to my first day:
and now I see the final one approach.

117

Time flies, and yet the woeful sufferer
to whom it's given to acquire virtue,
enduring fame and endless salvation,
does not know that its harm can't be undone;
yet lazily he forms within his mind
a pretext for his sloth and an excuse
for talent wasted, which, perceived too late,
he mourns forlornly, and repents in vain.

The little ant awakens with the sun
in summertime, and gathers up the food
that will sustain it in the hostile cold.
To one who's indolent it always seems
a strain: so then in wintertime he dies, or else
he begs, and often fishes with no line.

118

Fassi davanti a noi il sommo Bene
col gremb'aperto e pien de' suoi tesori,
ed, acciò che ciascun se n'innamori,
a monstrar quali e' son sovent'e' viene;
e de signor amico ne diviene,
s'aprir vogliàngli i nostri freddi cuori,
e spira quinci e quindi e santi ardori
a raffrenar le colpe e tôr le pene.

E noi, protervi, ritrosi e selvaggi,
ci ritraiam indrieto, ed al fallace
ben temporale ostinati crediamo:
dal quale menati per falsi vïaggi,
perdiàn, miseri noi!, l'eterna pace,
e nel foco perpetüo caggiamo.

119

Volgiti, spirto affaticato, omai,
volgiti, e vedi dove sei trascorso,
del desio folle seguitando 'l corso:
e col piè nella fossa ti vedrai!
Prima che caggi, svégliati! Che fai?
Torna a Colui il quale il ver soccorso
a chi vuol presta e libera dal morso
della Morte dolente, alla qual vai.

Ritorna a lui, e l'ultimo tuo tempo
concedi almeno al suo piacer, piangendo
l'opere mal commesse nel passato.
Né ti spaventi il non andar per tempo,
ch'ei ti riceverà, ver' te facendo
quel ch'e' già fece all'ultimo locato.

118

The highest Good presents itself to us
with open arms and bearing treasured goods,
and so that everyone might love these gifts
he comes time and again to make them known;
from master he becomes a friend to us,
if we unfolded our cold hearts to him,
and breathes his holy ardour everywhere
to curb our sin and lessen suffering.

And we, hubristic, disobedient
and wild, slip backwards, and persistently
believe that all false temporal good is true:
by being led on journeys that are false,
we lose, unhappy us!, eternal peace,
and fall into the everlasting fire.

119

Now turn yourself around, tired spirit, turn
yourself around and see where you have gone
by following the path of rash desire:
you'll see yourself with one foot in the grave!
Before you fall, wake up! What are you doing?
Return to Him who offers true relief
to those who seek it and will save them from
the sting of painful Death, towards which you rush.

Return to him, and in your final hours
at least grant him his wish, repenting for
the evil deeds you practised in the past.
Fear not that you have acted tardily,
for he'll receive you, doing for you what
he did already for the last hired hand.

120

O Sol ch'allumi l'un'e l'altra vita
e dentro al pugno tuo richiudi il mondo,
poi non ti parve grave il mortal pondo
per ritornarci nella via smarrita,
se pietos'orazion fu mai udita
ch'al ciel venisse a te da questo fondo,
a me, che 'l mio bisogno non ascondo,
presta i benign'orecchi e sì m'aita!

Io ho, seguendo gli terren' diletti
e i tuo comandamenti non curando,
offeso spesso la tua maiestade.
Or mi ravveggio, come tu permetti,
e di tuo corte mi conosco in bando:
però, di grazia, addomando pietade!

121

O glorïoso Re che 'l ciel governi
con eterna ragione, e de' mortali,
sol, conosci le menti, e quant'e quali
e nostri pensier' sien chiaro discerni,
deh, volgiti ver' me, se tu non sperni
gli umili prieghi, e l'affezion' carnali
da me rimuovi, e sì m'impenna l'ali
che io possa volare a' beni eterni!

Lieva dagli occhi mia l'oscuro velo
che veder non mi lascia lo mio errore,
e me sviluppa dal piacer fallace!
Caccia dal petto mio il mortal gelo,
e quell'accendi sì del tuo valore
che io di qui ne vegna alla tua pace!

120

O Sun, who shines on this and on the other
life and holds the whole world in its hand,
because our mortal weight seemed not too great
for you not to redeem us from being lost,
if you have ever heard a pious prayer
rise up to heaven from this world below,
lend me, for I do not conceal my need,
your gracious ear and thereby bring me help.

I have, in the pursuit of earthly joy
and paying your commandments little heed,
offended many times your majesty.
I now repent, as much as you permit,
and know that I am exiled from your court:
so, by your grace, I ask to have your mercy!

121

O glorious King, who governs heaven with
eternal justice, and who knows, alone,
the minds of mortal beings, and can discern
the nature of our thoughts with clarity,
ah, turn towards me, if you do not disdain
all humble prayers, and take away from me
all carnal lust and so empower my wings
that I may fly to everlasting good.

Lift from my eyes the veil that dims my sight
and blinds me to the error of my ways,
and liberate me from all false delight!
Cast from my heart my mortal iciness,
and with your worthiness set fire to it
so that from here I may attain your peace.

122

Non treccia d'oro, non d'occhi vaghezza,
non costume real, non leggiadria,
non giovanett'età, non melodia,
non angelico aspetto, né bellezza
poté tirar dalla sovran'altezza
il Re del cielo in questa vita ria
ad incarnar in te, dolce Maria,
Madre di grazia e specchio d'allegrezza;

ma l'umilità tua, la qual fu tanta
che poté romper ogn'antico sdegno
tra Dio e noi, e far il ciel aprire.
Quella ne presta adunque, Madre santa,
sì che possiamo al tuo beato regno,
seguendo lei devoti, ancor salire!

123

O luce eterna, o stella matutina
la qual chiuder non può Borea né Austro,
della nave di Pier timone, e plaustro
del biforme grifon che la divina
città lasciò per farsi medicina,
pria sé chiudendo nel virginal claustro,
del mal che già commise il protoplaustro
disubbidendo in nostra e sua rüina,

volgi gli occhi pietosi allo mio stato,
Donna del cielo, e non m'aver a sdegno
perch'io sia di peccati grave e brutto!
Io spero in te, e 'n te sempr'ho sperato:
prega per me, e esser mi fa' degno
di veder teco il tuo beato Frutto!

122

No golden tress, no splendour of the eyes,
no regal finery, no graciousness,
no youthful age, no harmony of sound,
no beauty or angelic countenance
could draw the King of heaven from his high
supremacy into this evil world
to incarnate in you, O sweet Maria,
Mother of grace and mirror of happiness,

except for your humility, which was
so great that it could quell the age-old spite
dividing God and us, and open heaven.
Thus, holy Mother, offer it to us
so we, in practising it dutifully,
may yet ascend into your hallowed realm!

123

O everlasting light, O morning star
that can't be hidden in the North or South,
the helm of Peter's ship, the wagon of
the biform gryphon that left heaven's realm
in order to become the remedy,
before enclosing itself in the virgin's womb,
for the sin our ancestor carried out
whose mutiny destroyed both us and it,

direct your eyes of pity on my state,
celestial Lady, don't disparage me
for being burdened and befouled by sin!
I place my hope in you and always have:
now pray for me, and make me capable
of being with you and seeing your blessed Fruit!

124

O Regina degli angioli, o Maria,
ch'adorni il ciel con tuoi lieti sembianti
e, stella in mar, dirizzi e naviganti
a port'e segno di diritta via,
per la gloria ove sei, Vergine pia,
ti prego guardi a' mia miseri pianti!
Incréscati di me! Tômi davanti
l'insidie di colui che mi travìa!

Io spero in te ed ho sempre sperato:
vagliami il lungo amore e 'l reverente
il qual ti porto e ho sempre portato.
Dirizza il mio cammin, fammi possente
di divenir ancor dal destro lato
del tuo Figliuol, fra la beata gente!

125

Tu mi trafiggi, ed io non son d'acciaio:
e s'a dir mi sospingon le punture
a dover ritrovarti le costure,
credo parratti desto un gran vespaio.
Deh, tu m'hai pieno, anzi colmo, lo staio!
Bastiti omai, perdio!, e non m'indure
a dettar versi delle tua lordure,
ch'io sarò d'altra foggia ch'io non paio!

E poi che la parola uscita è fuore,
indrieto ritornar non si può mai,
né vale il dir "Vorrei aver creduto!".
Se 'l ti prude la penna, il folle amore
e la fortuna dàn da dire assai:
in ciò trastulla lo tuo ingegno acuto.

124

O Queen of all the angels, O Maria,
adorning heaven with your happy mien,
star of the sea, directing mariners
to port and showing where the straight way lies,
I beg you, pious Virgin, for the glory
where you abide, to heed my wretched tears!
Have pity on me! Take away the snare
before me of the one who makes me stray!

I place my hope in you and always have:
may my long love avail me, and the awe
I bear for you which I have always borne.
Show me the way, and make me strong enough
to reach still even now the right-hand side
of your own Son, among the blessed ones.

125

You run me through, and I'm not made of steel:
and if my wounds compel me to respond
by giving you the beating you deserve,
I think you'll find you've stirred a hornet's nest.
Ah, not just far, you've gone beyond the pale!
For God's sake, that's enough now, and don't force
my hand to scribble verse about your filth,
for I'll adopt a tack you won't expect!

And since your words have seen the light of day,
they never can be taken back again,
nor can you say "I ought to have believed!"
So if your pen is itching in your hand,
mad love and fortune offer much to say:
amuse your biting intellect with that.

126

Poi satiro sei fatto sì severo
nella mia colpa, ed ètti sì molesta,
credo sarebbe cosa assai onesta
prima lavasse il tuo gran vitupèro
che mordesse l'altrui: uom sa, per vero,
la dolorosa e puzzolente festa
che festi del tuo nato, quand'in questa
vita 'l produsse il natural sentiero.

Né lascia questo divenire antiquo
l'infamia tüa, ché nel cinquantesmo
gravida avevi quella cui tenevi.
O crudel patre, o sacerdote iniquo,
poi, dov'uom scarca 'l ventre per battesmo
si died'a quel cui generato avevi!

127

Or sei salito, caro signor mio,
nel regno al qual salire ancor aspetta
ogn'anima da Dio a quell'eletta
nel suo partir di questo mondo rio.
Or se' colà dove spesso il desio
ti tirò già per veder Laüretta;
or sei dove la mia bella Fiammetta
siede con lei nel cospetto di Dio.

Or con Sennuccio e con Cino e con Dante
vivi, sicuro d'eterno riposo,
mirando cose da noi non intese.
Deh, s'a grado ti fui nel mondo errante,
tirami drieto a te, dove gioioso
veggia colei che pria d'amor m'accese!

126

Since you have ridiculed me so severely
for my faults, which trouble you so much,
I think that it would be an honest deed
if you first cleansed yourself for lashing out
in criticizing others: in fact, it's known,
that painful, odious act you carried out
upon your son, when nature's conduit
engendered him and he was brought to life.

Nor does becoming elderly remit
your infamy, for in your fiftieth year
you made the one you live with carry child.
O cruel father, O you wicked priest,
because where one unloads his guts was where
you baptized him to whom you'd given life!

127

You have ascended now, my dearest lord,
into the realm, which every soul aspires
to reach, of those elected by God's will,
in its departure from this evil world.
You're now where often the desire to see
Lauretta had already guided you;
you now are where my lovely Fiammetta
sits with her before the face of God.

You now dwell with Sennuccio and with Cino,
and Dante, certain of eternal rest,
and look on things we cannot understand.
Ah, if you loved me in the wayward world,
draw me behind you, where I happily
will see the one who first enamoured me!

Poems of Uncertain Attribution

1

Sì tosto come il sole a noi s'asconde
e l'ombra vien, che 'l suo lume ne toglie,
ogn'animale in Terra si racoglie
al notturno riposo, insin che l'onde
di Gange rendon con le chiome bionde
al mondo l'Aürora, e le lor doglie,
i duri affanni e l'amorose voglie
söave sonno allevia o le confonde.

Ma io, come si fa il ciel tenebroso,
sì gran pianto per gli occhi mando fore
che tant'acqua non versan dua fontane;
né dormir, né speranza alcun riposo
posson prestare al mio crudel dolore:
così m'affligge Amor fin la dimane.

2

L'aspre montagne e le valli profonde,
i folti boschi e l'acqua e 'l ghiaccio e 'l vento,
l' alpi selvagge e piene di spavento,
e de' fiumi e de' mar' le torbid'onde,
e qualunqu'altra cosa più confonde
il pover peregrin, che mal contento
da' sua s'allunga, non ch'alcun tormento
mi desser, tornand'io, ma fûr gioconde:

tanta dolce speranza mi recava,
spronato dal desio di rivederti
qual ver' me ti lasciai, donna, pietosa.
Or, oltra quel che io, lasso!, stimava,
truovo mi sdegni, e non so per quai merti:
per che piange nel cor l'alma dogliosa.

E maledico i monti, l'alpi e 'l mare,
che mai mi ci lasciaron ritornare.

1

As soon as the sun hides itself from us
and darkness falls, depriving us of light,
all animals on earth prepare themselves
to rest throughout the night until the waves
along the Ganges render to the world
the dawning of the day with golden locks,
and pleasant sleep alleviates or melts
their pain, distress, and thirst for love.

But I, just like a sky that's darkening,
release so great a torrent from my eyes
that so much water two founts could not yield;
and neither sleep nor hope can furnish me
with any respite from my cruel pain:
so does Love punish me right through to dawn.

2

The rugged mountains and the yawning vales,
the thick woods and the water, ice, and wind,
the savage peaks that prove so harrowing,
the murky waves of rivers and the sea,
and whatever else most preoccupies
the needy traveller, who unhappily
must leave behind his family, brought me
not only pain, but, coming back, some joy:

it gave me such sweet hope that I felt spurred
by the desire to see you once again
just as I'd left you, lady, kind towards me.
Beyond what I expected, I, alas!,
now find you scorn me, and I don't know why:
and so my grieving soul weeps in my heart.

I curse the mountains and the peaks and sea
that ever did allow me to return.

3

I cape' d'òr, di verde fronde ornati,
gli occhi lucenti e l'angelico viso,
i leggiadri costumi e 'l vago riso
di questa onesta donna hanno scacciati
tutti li mia disiri, e sono in atti
di sì somma biltà qual' io diviso,
ed hanno di lor fatto un paradiso
degli occhi mei, più ch'altri, innamorati.

Onde ogni altra bellezza m'è noiosa:
questa mi piace e questa vo cercando,
in questa ogni mia gioia si riposa.
Per lei sospiro e per lei vo cantando,
per lei m'aggrada la vita amorosa,
per lei salute spero disïando.

4

Prati, giardini, vaghi balli o canti,
sollazzi né diletti né piacere,
giovane adatt'e leggiadre vedere,
donne seguite da amorosi amanti,
nulla ne piace a me, quando davanti
non vegg'io nell'aspetto mio sedere
l'angelico bel viso al cui piacere
vive contento il cuor de' sua sembianti.
....

3

The golden hair adorned with verdant fronds,
the lucent eyes and the angelic face,
the graceful gestures and the lovely smile
of this praiseworthy lady have dispelled
all my desire, and they are traits that have
as much great beauty as I illustrate,
and of themselves they've made a paradise
to my enamoured eyes, more than to others.

Hence every other beauty's tedious:
I like this one and this one I seek out,
in this one all my joy finds its repose.
Because of her I sigh and sing love songs,
because of her my life of love brings joy,
because of my desire for her, I hope for bliss.

4

Not meadows, gardens, lovely dances, songs,
amusements nor delights nor merriment,
seeing talented and graceful girls
and ladies followed by their devotees,
none of this pleases me, when I don't see
in front of me being present in my sight
the lovely angel face of her whose beauty
makes my heart live in joy with her appearance.
....

5

La volontà più volte è corsa al core
per discoprire a coste' le mia pene:
la boce a mezzo il petto si ritiene,
la lingua tace e perde ogni sentore.
Di nuovo il cor ancor prende valore
per voler dire, e pur fra due mi tiene:
"Sì dirai; non dirai. Non; sì conviene,
se fedel servo sè tanto d'Amore".

Po' che la lingua e 'l cor perde l'ardire,
dite, occhi, vo', lagrimando, parole,
facendo certa lei sol quant'io l'amo,
e discovrite el mio tanto martìre.
El suo bel viso splende più che 'l sole;
e, quanto più la fuggo, più la bramo.

6

Gli occhi che m'hanno il cor rubato e messo
nella prigion d'Amore e lì legato
Disio e Gelosia hanno mandato
e Speranza e Paura a star con esso;
le quale, a lui tenendosi da presso,
or tristo el fanno, ed or parer beato,
or arder tutto, ed or tutto gelato,
or pianger, or cantare; e quest'è spesso.

Onde il girato in così fatti stremi
forte sì duole per tal confusione;
grida mercé, e, perché nulla vale,
alzato ha vela e posto mano a' remi
più volte già per uscir di prigione:
ma, alzato il vol, li son strappate l'ale.

5

My will has many times gone to my heart
to indicate to her my suffering:
my voice has been held back within my breast,
my tongue is silent and no longer feels.
My heart then finds the courage once again
to try to speak, yet it keeps me in doubt:
"It's yes; it's no; it doesn't help; it helps,
if you're a faithful devotee of Love."

Because the tongue and heart lose all their pluck,
eyes, speak, I want to hear words, as you cry,
convincing her just how much I love her,
and show the anguish of my suffering:
her lovely face is brighter than the sun;
the more I flee from her, the more I yearn.

6

My eyes have robbed my heart and placed it in
the prison house of Love and bound it there
and then dispatched Desire and Jealousy
with Hope and Fear to keep it company;
which, placing themselves very close to it,
make it now seem forlorn, then sanctified,
now all aflame, then wholly cold as ice,

now weeping, then in song, repeatedly.
Being turned about between such great extremes,
it feels deep pain from such ambivalence;
it calls for mercy, and, since that's no help,
it's raised a sail and put its hand to oars
already many times to flee from jail:
but, after taking flight, his wings are clipped.

7

Io mi credeä troppo ben l'altrieri
ricoverato aver mia libertate:
rotti avea i legami ed ispezzate
le porte ed ingannati i prigionieri,
e come per salvatichi sentieri
fuggiva forte e per vie disusate;
ma la sventura, che le mia pedate
seguì, <la> fece vani i mia pensieri.

Perciò ch'Amor, dond'io non avvisai,
vedendo mi rinchiude e, le sua armi
ver' me drizzando, gridò: "Tu sè giunto!
O fuggitivo servo, ove ne vai?".
Rider e 'l prender me e rilegarmi
e 'l darmi a' sua ministri fu in un punto.

8

I' ho già mille penne e più stancate
scrivendo in rima ed in parlar soluto
l'angoscioso dolor c'ho sostenuto
lunga stagione aspettando pietate.
E, s'io non erro, assai men quantitate
quietare il mar da' venti combattuto
e qualunqu'alto monte avrien dovuto
muover del luogo suo, men faticate,

non che 'l cuor d'una donna: il qual nïente
per lor di sua durezza s'è mutato,
ma stassi freddo come ghiaccio all'ombra.
Ond'io mi struggo, e dolorosamente
piango la mia fortuna disperato;
né 'l cuor, per tutto questo, non mi sgombra.

7

I thought I had most certainly regained
my liberty but not two days ago:
I'd torn away the bonds and broken down
the doors and taken in the prison guards,
and I was fleeing rapidly along
deserted paths and unfamiliar ways;
but misadventure, which was following
my tracks, made my thoughts meaningless.

For Love, from someplace where I hadn't looked,
seeing me, closed off my path, and, with his arms
extended right towards me, yelled: "You are caught!
O servile fugitive, where can you go?"
To laugh at me and seize and fasten me
and hand me to the guards came all at once.

8

I have worn out by now a thousand pens
or more describing both in verse and prose
the anguished pain that I have felt throughout
a very long time waiting for compassion.
And if I am not wrong, a lesser sum
by far would have sufficed to quiet down
a sea convulsed by winds and move as well
with less fatigue a lofty mountain from its base,

as well as, too, a woman's heart: which changed
its hardness not one jot because of them,
but kept its chilliness like ice in shade.
So now I tear myself apart and weep
most painfully about my hopeless lot;
in all of this, my heart can't free itself.

9

I' avea già le lagrime lasciate
e ritornava nel viso il colore,
perché alquanto più söave Amore
avea veduto, e l'arme avea posate.
Ed a bene sperar quella beltate
ch'al mondo non n'è par, non che maggiore,
m'invitava talor con lo splendore
che 'n inferno faria l'alme beate:

quando, per nuovo isdegno, mi trovai
senza ragion nel mio misero stato,
nel qual mi struggo, come neve al sole,
in pianti ed in sospiri, in doglia e 'n guai;
né a me gridar mercé, poscia, ha giovato
a chi pur morto, e non altro, mi vole.

10

I' solea spesso ragionar d'amore
e talora cantar del vago viso
del qual fatto s'avea suo paradiso,
come di luogo eletto, il mio signore.
Or è il mio canto rivolto in dolore
e trasmutato in pianto il dolce riso,
po' che per morte da no' s'è diviso
e terra è divenuto il suo splendore.

Né sarà mai ch'alla mente mi torni
quella imagine bella che conforto
porger solea a ciascun mio disire
che io non pianga e maladichi i giorni
che tanto m'hanno in questa vita scòrto
ch'io sento del mio ben fatto martìre.

9

I had already put aside my tears
and colour was returning to my face,
because I'd seen that Love was more benign
and had laid down the weapons he once used.
And to secure my hope, her loveliness,
which has no equal in the world, nor greater,
would tempt me sometimes with a radiance
that in inferno would save any soul:

and then, her scorn renewed, I found myself,
and for no reason, back in misery,
in which I melt, like snow beneath the sun,
in tears and sighs, and pain and wretchedness;
nor did it help to plead for mercy, then,
from one who wants me dead, and nothing less.

10

I used to speak of love quite frequently
and sometimes sing about the lovely face
of which my lord had made his paradise,
as his distinguished place of preference.
My song has now turned into a lament
and her sweet smile transmuted into tears,
since owing to her death it's been withdrawn
from us, and all her splendour's turned to dust.

And never will that lovely image chance
to reappear, which used to offer me
relief for every one of my desires
so that I would not cry and curse the days
that have led me through so much of my life
that I feel my joy has become my pain.

11

O ch'Amor sia, o sia lucida stella,
te nel mio meditar forma sovente
leggiadra, vaga, splendida e piacente,
qual viva esser solevi, e così bella.
Quivi con teco l'anima favella,
ode e risponde, e tanta gioia sente
che la gloria del ciel crede nïente,
quantunque grande, per rispetto a quella.

Ma com la viva imagine si fugge
e rompesi il pensier che la tenea
e che 'n terra sè cener mi ricorda,
torna il dolor che mi consuma e strugge,
e prego te che la Morte mi déa
di te seguir. Deh, non esser più sorda!

11

Whether Love or a resplendent star,
it often recreates you in my thoughts
as graceful, lovely, pleasing, marvellous,
and beautiful, as you were when alive.
Being here with you my soul can speak,
hear and reply, and it feels so much joy
that it regards the glory of heaven as naught,
however great, when it's compared with her.

But as soon as the living image flees
and so destroys the thought sustaining it
and I recall that she is ash in earth,
the pain returns to crush and ruin me,
and I beseech that Death give me consent
to follow you. Ah, be no longer deaf!

12

Nascosi son gli spirti e l'ombre tolte
di fronde agli albuscelli
dal poco amico inverno e da' suo nati:
ma non senza cagion le 'ngiurie molte
fatte gli son da quelli
per dargli maggior merti e più onorati.
Ma, s'io ben seguo gli amorosi stati,
di te è similitudo,
che con affanno e sudo
ha' con Amor più tempo conversato.
Or è tolto l'usato,
poi che la iddeä Pallàs t'ha promesso,
Venùs e Mars e Pallàs dier concesso!

Hanti fatto principio grazïoso
senza pigliar lunghezza
o altro tedio sopra tua procura.
Benché i' degno fosse a star nascoso,
tuo prudenza e bellezza
a me donato fu farne figura.
Ma ben ch'a me sia grave tal ventura,
per non disubbidire
all'amoroso sire
con riverenza acconterò gli onori
che ciascuna di fuori,
in disparte, ti fêr le dee amiche,
sì che onoralle possa in tuo rubriche.

Quella vezzosa dea Venùs, sorella
ch'è del vago Piacere,
Amor ti porse, nella prima vista,
nel viso di colei, leggiadra e snella.
Sempre ti pare avere
colorata, nel cor, d'amor suo lista
bench'io conosco in cui sempre s'attrista,
quando privasti il passo
col petto sodo e masso,
facendoli aüggiar *piazzinga* terra.
Sì che virtù disserra:
ché, prima ch'ogni onor fatto le sia,
di tal donna t'ha fatto cortesia.

12

The hidden spirits and the shade of fronds
are taken from the trees
by hostile winter and its elements:
but not for naught those many ravagings
were done to them by such
to give them greater worth and more esteem.
But, if I understand the states of love,
this does resemble you,
who with distress and sweat
have long performed the ritual of love.
That routine's over now,
because the goddess Pallas promised you,
and Venus, Mars, and Pallas gave you gifts!

They made a kind beginning helping you
without their wasting time
or having to have some dull pledge from you.
Though I was worthy to remain at bay,
it was bestowed on me
to represent your prudence and your beauty.
But while this venture may be hard for me,
so I don't disobey
the lord of love himself,
with reverence I shall reveal the honours
that, each one outwardly,
the friendly goddesses gave you in secrecy,
so you may honour them in what you write.

That comely goddess Venus, who's the sister
of passionate Delight,
presented Love to you, at your first sight,
within the face of her, who's fair and swift.
You always seem to have
a cheerful sign of her love in your heart,
though I know in whose heart that sign is sad,
when you cut off his path
with your hard massive form,
by ruining his fortified home town,
your virtue thereby shown,
since, before any honour's given her,
of such a woman she's made you a gift.

Invocar dèe, come fervente amico
delle battaglie, Marte,
sì come provvedente a più ragione:
ché comprese tuo mente, sì pudico
che ti rogò le carte
di quella armata, senza far quistione:
non facendo d'alcuno altro menzione,
ma difinendo, spero,
che in istato sincero
....

....

verrai della tua donna per prodezza,
tra pel suo senno e per l'altrui mattezza.

Mostrò Pallàde alla promessa grazia
fusse fervente e tosta,
con l'altre sue compagne, a farti onore.
Sì come imperïal suo veste spazia,
e suo corona ha posta
sopra la vaga donna, ch'ha 'l tuo core.
Po' l'usate ricchezze trasse fore
dal lor padrone antico,
ed a te, come amico,
ligittimolle; e tu il passo largisti
con vaghi color' misti.
Questa beata dea nudritti a guisa
che sempre dèi portar la sua divisa.

Dolce canzon, per cui suggetto stato
son notti e giorni alquanti,
vanne a colui per cui mi ti fe' servo.
Te gli offerrai sì come il più onorato,
e me a' prossimanti
gli dona come amico col tuo verbo;
e di' che mi gli serbo
sì come amico in segreto e 'n palese,
qual fen le dee che preson sue difese.

You must appeal to Mars, the passionate
protagonist of war,
as being with greater reason well prepared:
because he understood your mind, so honest
that he drew up the plan
for that assault, without a question asked:
not making any other reference,
but clarifying, I hope,
that in sincerity
....

....

you will approach your lady through great feats,
through his insight and through another's folly.

Pallas signaled to the promised love
that she be keen and quick
to honour you, with all her other friends.
She billows her attire so as to look
imperial, and crowned
the lovely lady's head who holds your heart.
Then she brought out her celebrated wealth
from their long-standing lord,
and then to you, as friend,
she transferred it; and you bestowed the way
with many lovely hues.
This happy goddess cared for you and showed
how you must bear her emblem at all times.

Sweet song, with which I've occupied myself
for many days and nights,
find him for whom I made myself your aide.
Bestow yourself on the most honoured one,
and give me as his friend
to those nearby with thanks for what you've said;
and say that I'll keep him
as my friend both in private and in public,
as do the goddesses who favoured him.

13 L'*Ave Maria*

La dolce *Ave Maria* di grazia *plena,*
Dominus tecum, la qual fu salute
che 'l primo fallo e noi trasse di pena,
acciò ch'al mio prencipio die virtude,
com'e' bisogna, perché l'alma viva
fuor di miseria e delle genti crude,
divoto priego ch'alla vaga riva
di coscïenza, con pietà rassegna,
guidi la barca mia di porto schiva;
e scaldimi del Sol ch'eterno regna,
lo qual risplende in ciaschedun cristiano,
che solo in dargli tre palme s'assegna.
La prima delle qual' sia il senso umano,
mostrar del suo peccar contrito core,
con occhio lagrimoso e spirto sano.
Seconda sïa in confessar l'errore
c'ha sotto volontà posto el talento,
né, perch'e' grave sia, farlo minore.
La terza sïa in disïar contento,
lo confessato e lo pentuto fallo
purgar con opra, e poi tenerlo spento.
E quest'è 'l bianco e meritato callo,
quest'è 'l diletto del giusto appetito
che degno canta nel beato ballo.
Dinnanzi a queste non vince partito
la fiera lupa delle sette branche,
con le quai <sì> artiglia il più romito.
Quest'è superbia, avarizïa ed anche
lussuria, invidia e la bramosa gola,
ira e accidia, ch'avverar son franche.
Di fuor si mostran vaghe sì, che 'nvola
dall'intelletto nostro l'occhio pio,
dal buon rispetto ch'al superno vola.
L'umana sorte fa di lor disio,
onora e loda chi n'ha maggior soma
e piglia maggior' pesci di tal rio,
senza rispetto di Colui che doma
con l'alta chiova ogni animal feroce
e che ci scorse alle vietate poma,

13 *Ave Maria*

Sweet *Ave Maria*, who is full of grace,
Dominus tecum, which was deliverance
that removed the first sin and us from pain,
so that it gives me power as I begin,
it being required, for my soul to exist
apart from suffering and the debased,
I pray devoutly that at the fair shore
of conscience, with pity measured out,
you will guide my reluctant boat to port;
and warm me with the Sun that reigns eternal,
which shines on each and every Christian soul
and only must provide each with three palms.
The first of these is known as human feeling,
to show contrition in the heart for sins,
with tearful eyes and spiritual well-being.
The second is confession of one's sin,
which was to place the will beneath desire,
and not, however grave, to lessen it.
The third is taking pleasure in contempt,
and purging with good works the sin that was
repented and confessed, with no relapse.
This is the path that's meritorious
and pure, this is delight from just desire
that sings most justly in the dance of heaven.
Against these guarantees the savage wolf
with seven limbs can never win, with which
he sets his claws on the least culpable.
These make up pride and avarice and lust,
then envy and voracious gluttony,
and wrath and sloth, so likely to occur.
They seem enchanting outwardly so as
to steal the pious eye from reason's sway,
from feelings that are pointed heavenward.
The human kind desires only them,
it honours and it praises those who have
much more and take more fish from such a stream,
without regard to Him who subjugates
on high ground every feral living being
and who led us to the forbidden fruit,

lasciandosi per noi por nella croce,
ferir e fragellar fin nella morte
ch'al *Consummatum est* aperse voce;
dalla qual risurgendo, spezzò porte
del scuro Limbo, scarcerando quegli
che degni ritrovò per giusta sorte.
E montando nel ciel, lasciò a noi i gigli
delli Apostoli suoi, che fêro al mondo
la via che drizza agli eterni consigli:
col Padre e Spirto Santo è Quel giocondo,
e Elli in Lui, sicché son tre in uno,
e uno in Trinità indiviso e tondo.
Ivi è giustizia senza manco alcuno;
iv'è misericordia e valor tutto,
che merita di noi il bianco e 'l bruno.
Ivi è la Madre di quel dolce Frutto
che con piatade sempre grazia acquista
alla miseria d'esto mondo brutto;
a cu' 'ntendo di drizzar mia vista
con le dolci parole di colui
che nanzi al nascer suo fu profetista.
Lo qual gli disse, com fu innanzi a lui:
"*Benedicta tu in mulïeribus,*
et benedictus fructus ventris tui,
– flettendo sé 'n *Helisabeth visceribus* –,
et unde mihi hoc, che El me vène
a visitar, *pre ceteris muneribus,*
la Madre del Signor d'ogni mio bene?"
finendo qui la vera profezia
ch'al grembo verginal raffermò spene.
Così io, con fedele melodia,
dico: "O sòpra tutte benedetta,
per Spirto Santo eletta Madre pia
del benedetto Frutto che in distretta
del ventre tuo si pose, finch'El nacque
e prese carne umana, pura e netta!
S'io ben comprendo, tu sè il mar dell'acque
che drizzan corso per lo sommo regno,
e sè ciò che 'n valor virtù compiacque.
Tu sè la fede dello cristian segno,
tu sè speranza al giusto e al peccatore,
e sè di carità perfetto ingegno.

agreeing to be placed on the cross for us,
be flogged and wounded right up to His death,
at which He uttered "*Consummatum est*";
from which, restored to life, He broke the gates
of lightless Limbo, setting free all those
whom He found worthy of being justly saved.
And rising up to heaven, He left to us
the lilies of His Apostles, who gave the world
the way that leads to the eternal counsel:
that joyous One joins Father and the Spirit,
and They join Him, so that the three are one,
and the one conjoined with the Trinity.
There is justice with no deficiency;
there is mercy and complete worthiness,
which justifies the light and dark in us.
There is the Mother of that pleasing Fruit
who always metes out grace with sympathy
for those in need in this unpleasant world;
to whom I now mean to address my thought
with words of sweetness spoken by the one
who was a prophet before he was born.
He said to him, when he'd drawn near his side:
"*Benedicta tu in mulieribus,*
et benedictus fructus ventris tui,
kneeling in *Helisabeth visceribus* –,
et unde mihi hoc, why did God come
to visit me, *pre ceteris muneribus,*
the Mother of the Lord of every good?,"
the true prophecy culminating here,
confirming the hope in the virgin's womb.
And so then I, with faithful melody,
declared: "O blessed above all other women,
pious Mother chosen by the Holy
Spirit of the blessed Fruit that placed Himself
within the furrow of your womb, till God
was born with human flesh, she pure and clean!
If I well understand, you are the sea
of waters that flow through the highest realm,
and what fulfilled true virtue with your worth.
You are the faith of the Christian standard,
you are the hope for sinners and the just,
you are the perfect means of charity.

'N te è sapienza, in te prudente fiore,
in te intelletto, in te magnificenza
e magnanimità con grande amore.
Tesor sè sommo di somma prudenza;
la qual soccorri ispesso innanzi al prego
a chi ti porta, com dea, reverenza.
Non è benignità che non sie teco;
non è umilità, né tenerezza,
non è perfetto ben stu non sè seco.
Tu sè splendor di superna chiarezza,
diletto incomprensibil di quel trono
che canta *Osanna* nell'eterna altezza.
Ciò che tu daï è perfetto dono,
né mai sdegni l'udire a chi ti chiama,
né pagan, né giudeo, s'e' vuol perdono,
perché sempre sè verde e ferma rama,
alla qual chi s'appiglia mai non cade,
e sempre prieghi per ciascun che t'ama.
Ond'io, o donna, o fonte di pietade,
ben ch'io fra ' peccator' grave mi senta,
vegno divoto alla tua maestade;
e con il core e colla mente intenta
in tutto a te confesso il mio peccare,
che sanza freno cavalcar contenta,
lasciandomi più volte incatenare,
per gran lascività, lo mie intelletto;
e dov'e' più conosce, è più fallace,
pigliando di malizia ogni diletto.
Né mai d'altrui miseria a coscïenza
guardo, ovver<o> dimostro aver rispetto;
d'ogni vergogna certo ho sperïenza,
senza memoria delle somme scale,
né mai la mente drizzo a penitenza.
E 'l bianco e 'l biondo e l'aver criminale
involgon vaga mia fatica e voglia,
e a me paion virtù cardinale!
Lo mio arbitrio di virtù si spoglia:
non vegg'io, senza te, che mai l'adorna
e santa corte tra lor me raccoglia.
Però, Vergine eccelsa, in cui soggiorna
ciò che 'n *excelsis* lo tuo Figlio onora
ed odi il *Miserere* ch'a te torna,

In you is wisdom, and the flower of prudence,
in you are intellect, magnificence
and magnanimity with noble love.
You are the greatest wealth of highest prudence,
which you bring often prior to the prayer
to one who bears you reverence, as goddess.
There is no loving-kindness without you;
there's no humility, nor tenderness,
no perfect good unless you are with it.
You are the splendour of supernal light,
inscrutable delight of that high throne
that sings *Osanna* in the timeless dome.
Whatever you give is a perfect gift,
you won't refuse to hear appeals to you,
not pagan, nor Jew, if a pardon's sought,
because you are the fresh and steady bough
from which no one can fall who holds on tight,
and always pray for those who love you well.
So I, O Lady, pity's fountainhead,
although I feel myself weighed down by sins,
I come devoutly to your majesty;
and with my heart and mind resolved
completely I confess to you my sins,
which like to charge ahead without restraint
and make me frequently restrain, because
of great licentiousness, my intellect;
the more it knows, the more it goes astray,
by taking great delight in wickedness.
I never give thought to another's grief,
nor do I ever show respect for anyone;
I certainly have felt all kinds of shame,
without remembering the lofty stairs,
and I don't ever think of penitence.
The white and blonde, as well illicit wealth,
comprise my errant work and wayward will,
yet cardinal virtues they appear to me!
My freewill keeps all virtue far away:
deprived of you, I don't see how I can
join them within the lovely, holy court.
And so, exalted Virgin, in whom dwells
that which honours your Son *in excelsis*
and you hear the *Miserere* in response,

ricevi il priego mio, ch'a fé t'adora;
e come tu dicesti: "Ecco l'ancilla",
così mi scalda del tuo foco ognora, 126
lo quale in carità tanto sfavilla
ch'attuta e vince li furor' mondani,
e tocca il cor con divina scintilla. 129
Drizza la mente mia a quelli arcani
consigli e spirti che l'anima affetta,
e più la traë de' viluppi umani. 132
Non mi lasciar l'error che doman spetta,
e mi da' penitenza e confessione
perché sùbita vien mortal barchetta. 135
Cancella in me la falsa oppinïone:
dàmmi ch'i' pianga e contrito sospiri
gli mie trapassi e gravi offensïone. 138
Dàmmi diletto di sentir martirî
di mia malizia e di mia acerba possa,
e di seguir col cor li tuoi disiri. 141
Non mi lasciar tener mia colpa grossa;
dàmmi franchezza tal, ch'i' la discolpi,
com'e' bisogna a sì feroce mossa. 144
Non consentire all'insidiose volpi
gli agguati doppi ch'all'anima mia
han posti e pongon ché foco la spolpi. 147
Poi quando a Dio parrà che 'l mio fin sia,
perdon ti cheggio e che per mia vittoria
sempre la faccia tua nante mi stia; 150
la qual discacci quel ch'inferno storia
e me conservi così fermamente
com'e' bisogna ad acquistar la gloria
del tuo Figliuolo e Padre onnipotente". 154

receive my prayer, which lauds you faithfully;
and because you said 'Behold the handmaid,'
so is my heart warmed always with your fire,
which shines so greatly with your charity
it quells and overcomes all worldly rage,
and strikes the heart with sparks that are divine.
Direct my mind to that profound advice
and spirits which the soul so strongly craves,
and curb it more from human tendencies.
Hold back from me the error due to come,
and give me penance and let me confess
because the boat of death is coming soon.
Eradicate from me my false beliefs:
let me bemoan and mourn regretfully
my excesses and serious misdeeds.
Give me delight in feeling agony
for my ill will and cruel temperament,
and with my heart to follow your desire.
Keep me from clinging to my heavy sin;
make me hold firm in expiating it,
as is required of such malicious deeds.
Do not allow the foxes of deceit
deceptive traps which they have laid and lay
before my soul so that fire burns it up.
Then when it seems to God my end is near,
I ask for pardon and that your face be
before me always as my victory.
Let it dispel the schemes that hell creates,
and safeguard me as steadfastly as must
occur in order to acquire the glory
of your Son and Father omnipotent.

14

A dir che siate bella
scemo le vostre lode,
madonna, e mi riprende ognun che m'ode.
Nome non ci è conforme a quel che sête;
non so che cosa avete
più dell'uman, più del divin ancora:
li capegli d'aurora,
gli occhi del sole e 'l volto della luna.
E se bellezza alcuna
imaginar si può che non si vede,
chiar si dimostra in voi ch'ogni altra eccede:
né più bella di voi esser potria
Beltà, s' avesse forma, o Leggiadria.

15

Cresce la *fiamma* mia pur ch'io vi miri,
o mio bel sol, da cui mia vita pende,
né luce altra per me fra noi risplende
tosto ch'avièn ch'in voi questi occhi giri.
E fiano eterni gli alti miei desiri
sì come eterno è il ben ch'il cor m'incende:
santo amor ch'a sì degno obietto intende
alzar la mente e movere i sospiri.

Come, dunque, che scemi o per nuova ésca
in me fuoco d'amor s'accenda mai
nel pensier vostro sì gran dubio nacque?
Torbidi e freddi avrà ben prima i rai
il sol che quell'ardor del petto m'èsca
a cui me stesso consacrar mi piacque.

14

To say you're beautiful,
I, lady, underplay
your praise, and all who hear me censure me.
No word can correspond to what you are;
I don't know what you have
that's more than human, more, too, than divine:
locks of the golden dawn,
eyes of the sun and visage of the moon.
And if you can imagine
a loveliness that never has been seen,
it's clearly seen in you to transcend all:
and Beauty and Gentility, in flesh
and bone, could not be lovelier than you.

15

My *flame* grows even as I gaze on it,
O my fair sun, on whom my life depends,
nor can another light between us shine
as soon as my eyes turn to look at you.
And may my great desire last evermore
just like the good that burns within my heart:
it's holy love that's meant to raise the mind
and move one's sighs to such a worthy end.

How, then, was such profound doubt born in you
to fear my love for you should ever wane
or that it should flare up for someone else?
The sun's rays surely will grow dark and cold
before the ardour in my heart leaves me
to which I liked to consecrate myself.

16

Amor, che l'alme sì congiungi e i cori
che sol un cor e un'alma son gli amanti,
Amor, che gli aspri affanni e i rei dolori
rivolger fai in piacer, seccare i pianti,
Amor, ch'accendi con söavi ardori
i freddi petti e spezzi gli adamanti,
<lo spirto> intenerisci, accend<i amori>
al duro cor che mi dà <tremor' tanti>.
....

17

Mentre virtù de' bei vostri occhi sente,
arde ogn'alma gentil d'onesto amore,
tanto e sì puro è il lor vivo splendore,
il qual basso desir mai non consente.
Le voci, poi, se con l'orecchie intese
dall'angelica bocca ode uscir fore,
a voi sola volgendo i sensi e il core,
tutta d'alti pensier' s'empie la mente.

Ogni vostro atto con mirabil arte
l'anime lega e rende l'uom felice:
oh grazia altrui non data in Terra mai!
Ma chi rimira la divina parte
è fatto cieco al fine, e seco dice:
"In sole ardente, lasso, m'affissai!".

16

Love, you who bring together hearts and souls
so lovers can be just one heart and soul,
Love, you who turn harsh anguish and cruel pain
to pleasure and dry up the tears of woe,
Love, you who set on fire the frozen heart
with tender passion and break diamonds up,
assuage my spirit, set on fire the love
in my hard heart that makes me tremble so.
....

17

As long as it feels power from your fair eyes
a noble soul will burn with honest love,
so great and pure their radiance shines forth,
which never will consent to base desire.
If, then, with open ears it hears such words
as issue forth from your angelic mouth,
directing just towards you its mind and heart,
the mind is wholly filled with noble thoughts.

Every act of yours with wondrous skill
enthralls the soul and brings one happiness:
oh, grace no other ever earned on Earth!
But one who looks upon divinity
goes blind, at last, and utters to himself:
"Alas, I looked upon a burning sun!"

18

Oh come son talora
maravigliosi in noi,
Amor, gl'incendî tuoi!
Con accorciato crin, succinta in gonna,
innamorata donna
seguì del suo fedel l'orme leggiadre
fra bellicose squadre.
Ma così gran valore
nelle donne moderne or non si vede,
ché, s'han maggior bellezza, han minor fede.

19

Carissimi fratei, la forma oscura
di me misero teschio risguardate:
le mie bellezze son da me cascate;
son rimaso ombra di crudel figura!
Non men di voi fui già bella istatura:
e le mie membra son da me iscacciate
e dalli vermin' si son divorate,
di cui tutti saremo lor pastura.

Rigido peccatore, in me te specchia
e sappi come a me hai a tornare
<e> di bona armatura or ti coverchia!
Fal tosto, ché dubbioso è lo indugiare:
....
....
Chi séguita el mal fare
la Morte li conduce e falli stretta:
e sì è più forte che d'arco saetta.

18

Oh, how wonderful
your fervour burns in us,
now and again, lord Love!
With hair cut short, attired quite skimpily,
a woman who's in love
pursued the fair footprints of her true love
among the warring troops.
But valour such as this
in modern women is not seen these days,
for while more beautiful, they have less faith.

19

My dearest brothers, behold the morose
shell of this wretched skull of mine I bear:
my pleasing looks have fallen by the way;
I'm left the outline of a cruel shape!
No less than you I had a fair form once:
and now my limbs are torn away from me
and every one of them devoured by worms,
for which each one of us must serve as food.

Unbending sinner, see yourself in me
and know that you must be turned into me
and shield yourself now with a coat of mail!
Now do it soon, delay is dangerous:
....
....
Those who keep doing evil deeds
are led by Death who brings about their end:
and he's more potent than an arrow shot.

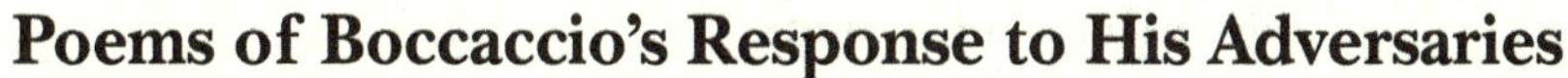

Poems of Boccaccio's Response to His Adversaries

1

S'io ho le Muse vilmente prostrate
nelle fornice del vulgo dolente,
e le lor parte occulte ho palesate
alla feccia plebeia scioccamente,
non cal che più mi sien rimproverate
sì facte offese, perché crudelmente
Appollo nel mio corpo l'ha vengiate
in guisa tal, ch'ogni membro ne sente.

Ei m'ha d'huom facto un otre divenire,
non pien di vento ma di piombo grave
tanto, ch'appena mi posso mutare.
Né spero mai di tal noia guarire,
sì d'ogni parte circondato m'have;
ben so però che Dio mi può aiutare.

2

Se Dante piange, dove ch'el si sia,
che li concetti del suo alto ingegno
aperti sieno stati al vulgo indegno,
come tu di', della lettura mia;
ciò mi dispiace molto, né mai fia
ch'io non ne porti verso me disdegno;
come ch'alquanto pur me ne ritegno,
perché d'altrui, non mia, fu tal follìa.

Vana speranza e vera povertade
e l'abbagliato senno delli amici
e gli lor prieghi ciò mi fecer fare.
Ma non goderan guar di tal derrate
questi ingrati meccanici, nimici
d'ogni leggiadro e caro adoperare.

1

If I have basely vilified the Muses
in the brothels of the wretched horde
and foolishly revealed their hidden parts
to loathsome commoners of little worth,
there is no further need for me to be
rebuked for such offenses, given that
Apollo has avenged them in my body
in such a way that each limb aches with pain.

He's turned me from a man into a bag,
full not of air but of such heavy lead
that I can barely move about at all.
Nor have I hope that I'll be healed of pain,
so completely it's enveloped me;
yet I well know that God can succour me.

2

If Dante grieves, wherever he may be,
that concepts of his lofty intellect
have been revealed to the unworthy horde,
as you have said, by readings I have made,
I feel remorse; and let it not be said
that I do not berate myself for this,
though I restrain myself somewhat because
such folly's owed to others and not me.

Vain hope and poverty that's genuine
and the unseeing judgment of my friends
and their entreaties have made me do this.
But these ungrateful artisans, true foes
of every graceful and fine industry,
will scarcely take joy in such merchandise.

3

Già stanco m'hanno e quasi rintuzzato
le rime tua accese in mia vergogna;
e quantunque a grattar della mia rogna
io abbia assai nel mio misero stato,
pur ho tal volta, da quelle sforzato,
risposto a quel che la tua penna agogna,
la qual non fu temperata a Bologna,
se ben ripensi il tuo aspro dettato.

Detto ho assai che io cruccioso sono
di ciò che stoltamente è stato fatto,
ma frastornarsi non si puote omai.
Però ti posa ed a me da' perdono,
ch'io ti prometto ben che 'n tal misfatto
più non mi spingerà alcun giammai.

4

Io ho messo in galea senza biscotto
l'ingrato vulgo, e senza alcun piloto
lasciato l'ho in mare a lui non noto,
bench'e' se 'n creda esser maestro e dotto:
onde il dì sù spero veder di sotto
del debol legno e di sanità vôto;
né avverrà, perch'ei sappia di nuoto,
ch'e' non rimanga lì doglioso e rotto.

Ed io, di parte eccelsa riguardando,
ridendo, in parte piglierò ristoro
del ricevuto scorno e dell'inganno;
e tal fïata a lui rimproverando
l'avaro seno ed il beffato alloro,
gli crescerò e la doglia e l'affanno.

3

They've more or less demeaned and wearied me,
your verses that were meant to bring me shame;
and although I have much to scratch the itch
I live with in this wretched state of mine,
I still, from time to time, compelled by them,
have answered what your pen demands of me,
which was not sharpened in Bologna's style,
if you give thought to your harsh idiom.

I've said enough about how I am vexed
by what has foolishly been said and done,
but this can be no longer taken back.
So, therefore, let it pass and pardon me,
for I can promise you I'll never be
led to offend in such a way again.

4

I've put the thankless rabble in a ship
with no provisions, and abandoned them
without a pilot in an unknown sea,
though they think they are crafty and astute:
and so I hope to see their fragile ship
turned upside down, so no one can be saved;
this won't occur, since they know how to swim,
for they won't stay there worn out and forlorn.

And I, who look down from a lofty place,
will take some comfort, laughing, from the scorn
that I've received and from their treachery;
and sternly reprimanding them at times
for greediness and having mocked the laurel,
I'll increase both their anguish and their pain.

Notes

Rime

1

Her choice of gentle words and her sweet smile

Boccaccio's lyrics employ the lexicon, style, and conceits of the poets of the *stilnovismo,* or *dolce stil novo* (sweet new style). The expressions "sweet smile" (1) and "golden tresses" (2) are topoi of the tradition, as is "eternal bliss" (11), a technical expression shared by both the stilnovists and Petrarch, meaning "paradise." The oxymoronic nature of love as instilled in the lover by the beauty of the beloved – which slays (3) him, yet restores him to life – is a fundamental characteristic of Boccaccio's poetry, as well as that of Petrarch and the stilnovists.

2

It often happens when I'm lost in thought

The poet imagines the image of the beloved entering his thoughts and taking possession of them, capturing his spirits and speaking to them of the qualities of the beloved, which bring both pleasure and a desire to act virtuously.

5 "my salvation": echoes Guinizzelli (*Rime* 10.10) and Dante (*Vita nova* 10, 21, 39; *Rime* 69.9).

18 "pulls towards itself": that is, the "celestial face" of the beloved pulls all of her inner spirits towards itself.

3

While I am gazing on you, beautiful

The sweetness of the beloved, whose beauty is uniquely supreme on earth, drives from the poet's heart all evil passions and enables him to recover his morale.

4

With how much tenderness I gaze on you

The sonnet accentuates the interplay of the eyes of the poet and those of the beloved. Her eyes have the power to fill his heart with hope, while his eyes have the power to draw sighs from hers, a gift that would mitigate his love suffering.

7 "that day": the day on which the poet fell in love with Fiammetta. Her name will appear in later lyrics.

5

So sweetly Love entraps me in his snares

Love, namely the god of love, Cupid, imprisons the lover, taking complete control of his amatory experience, empowering the eyes of the beloved to both drive him away and attract him. Love's radiance enlightens his heart (14), that is, it enkindles love in his heart and sets his heart on fire.

6

Now many who are crude disparage Love

The theme of defining the nature and effects of love is a classic topos taken up by Giacomo da Lentini, the founder of the Sicilian school of poetry and among the first to write in an Italian vernacular.

2 "accident": a scholastic term signifying an experience of an entity or a quality of a circumstance.

4 "lavish donor": the term, meaning "liberal," is used ironically here, whereas in verse 11 "cortese" has its usual sense of "polite" or "courteous."

7

This fire of love's so pleasant that I burn

The sonnet describes the oxymoronic nature of love in a series of antitheses, characterized by the classic metaphor of the phoenix that dies only to be reborn again from its own ashes.

5 "She": Fiammetta, the poet's beloved.

8

The spirit that is full of graciousness

The genesis of the poet's love, inspiring the hope of endless happiness, is beset by an unspecified fear that leads to an awareness of the brevity of life. The phrase "viver corto" (13) recalls Petrarch's *Canzoniere* 15.6.

9

Unhappy me! for I don't dare to look

The poet imagines conversing with the spirit of his lady. The initial happiness of the poet-lover followed by the fear of losing the lady echoes the theme of Dante's *Vita nova.*

10

When the enemy of love and mercy

The poet's enemy and the source of his torment is his unnamed cruel mistress, Fiammetta, who takes pleasure in persecuting him. She hopes to gain greater fame (8) through his poetry, which speaks of her. Despite his suffering, he hopes his fortune will improve, that "perse will turn to white" (12). Perse is a dark purple verging on black. The subject of the main clause in the first octave, unusually deferred, is "my heart" (7).

11

When can I hope my lady will one day

The desire to see the beloved in a dream is a traditional feature of Italian love poetry. The question raised at the beginning of the *rima* is sarcastically answered in the negative by the poet, leading him to desire death.

12 "those lights": the lady's eyes.

12

Some birds are so attracted to the light

The sonnet presents an analogy between birds attracted to light and the lover's attraction to his lady. Branca calls attention to the careful correlation of parts in the parallel set up in verses 10–12: "*voler* (*desio* 6), *drieto* (*drieto* 8), *begli occhi* (*picciol lume* 5), *occhi falsi* (*falso duce* 8), *nuove catene* (*sopposti lacci* 7–8)" (Branca, *Rime,* 239).

13

My tears and sighs and not expecting them

The topic of the lover's suffering, which instills in him a desire to reveal its cause (verses 1–11) as a way of gaining relief, takes up both quatrains and the first tercet. The second tercet reverses that forceful flow and ends, as it were, with a whimper. Boccaccio often structures his *rime* on a sudden reversal of events, a turning point, or peripeteia. It serves to create drama (and express meaning) within the limited area of a sonnet's fourteen verses, and often turns on the adversative "but."

14
Had I sufficient talent to describe

If he were able to reveal his lady's virtues and her cruelty towards him, he would describe how surprising it is that he is still alive given the "error on her part" (6; that is, cruelty) and the error on his part (unreasonable fidelity to her). Since he can't, he will simply state that his pain is greater than what he shows outwardly on his face and in his poetry.

15
If only what I say were understood

The opening verses express the poet's wish that his lady could understand his words as well as his "ardent" (2) sighs understand them; this, despite his suffering, would make his tears joyful. But in declaring to her – "to the one whom I'd wish" (6) – how much he suffers, his anguish would not last for very long and would be reduced.

14 "so hard a path": the path to reach his lady.

16
Although, because you have departed now

The theme of the lady's temporary absence occasioned by a departure in this and the next two sonnets is a topos of courtly poetry. It is the classic form of separation. In a kind of twist, her departure and failure to return becomes the poet's departure.

17
Ever since my eyes have lost the sight

The lady's departure causes the poet's soul to depart from his heart, bringing pain that cannot be "expressed by rules of art" (8) – that is, a pain that no poet, however skilled, would be able to expess.

1–2 "the sight / that is so fair": the sight of Fiammetta.

18
Alas, how sad is my adversity

Despite his lady's absence, the poet can at least conjure up her image in his memory, which brings pleasure – that is, until he remembers how far away she is. His amatory experience is a constant ebb and flow of feelings.

5 "the image": that of Fiammetta.

19
O my unhappy eyes more than all else

When his eyes first saw his lady's eyes, they brought anguish to his soul because she scorned it. His continued looking at her brings renewed pain. Now he hopes his eyes will weep even more heavily so as to purge them of her image and fend off yet some new love that would deceive him.

20
Some claim, distraught, it's fortune that's averse

Once again the eyes are the cause and culprit of the lover's misfortune. The *rima*'s inflection point occurs in verse 9, which counters the catalogue of previous examples of misfortune.

11 "flame": a word and image that evoke the name of Fiammetta.

21
May you be captured, Love, and tied in bonds

A stern *vituperium*, or reproach, of Cupid, and a traditional form in medieval literature, typical of Cecco Angiolieri's poetry in particular. This style stresses realism and the spirit of *poesia giocosa*, or *poesia comico-realistica*, as a response to the conventional themes of serious love poetry. Note that the first verse reverses the convention of Love tying the lover in bonds.

22
If I believed that during those five years

We know that Boccaccio's love affair began on 30 March 1336. The suggestion that it covered a period of five years is unfounded. Juxtaposing the "wasted time" (7) of his love for Fiammetta marks the advent of its end (verses 10 and 14).

23
O wicked man, O servant most disloyal

The poet imagines Fiammetta defending herself against his accusations directed at her in his lyrics.

24
No one, for being in a state of pain

The poet celebrates "his triumph over Fiammetta and Love" (Lanza, *Le Rime*, 48), which exemplifies the maxim that one should never lose hope, however slight it may be.

25

My sighs, be gone with you, my cries, be gone

Fiammetta finally recompenses her lover with the gift of her "saluto" (12), her greeting, the conventional stilnovist *guerdon* ("reward" in Old French), and what embodies the goal of Dante's love of Beatrice in the *Vita nova.*

26

Love, if this lady is not insincere

Fiammetta, overcome with emotion, appears ready to give herself to her lover. Love still punishes him with the fire of passion – "burned / inside your kiln" (12–13), the possessive pronoun linking with the vocative in verse 1 – but since Fiammetta takes pleasure in his passion, he thinks he perhaps ought to continue burning.

27

If the serpent that protects my treasure

The theme of the lover's scorn for his lady's husband, who jealously surveils her, is a topos of Occitan poetry. The lover's "tesoro" (1) is the husband's wife, the "serpente" (1) the husband or relative of the wife.

9 Mercury is the god, recruited by Jupiter, who lulls to sleep the hundred-eyed watchman Argos by telling the story of Pan's attempted seduction of Syrinx.

28

The splendour of your eyes, which sets my heart

Lanza remarks that this sonnet initiates a shift in Boccaccio's poetry away from mere imitation of the stilnovist style towards a manner of expression that he terms "late Gothic," which emphasizes the theme of death and the pairing of terror and pleasure (Lanza, *Le Rime,* 56).

29

If that flame *which has set my heart afire*

The flame in the first verse of this and the following three sonnets, encoding the identity of Fiammetta, is the central metaphor of each. It appears that Boccaccio designed each first verse so that the word "flame" would occupy a different position – beginning, middle, and end. This pattern exists, of course, only if we accept Lanza's ordering of the poems.

13 "consuming it with pain": his heart, the lyric's subject announced in the first verse.

30
When that flame *first began to blaze in me*

To emphasize the idea of the lover's passion, Boccaccio employs only two rhyme words in the octave, "fiamma" and "arde," while retaining the conventional rhyme scheme in the sestet. Its three rhyme words – "foco," "pianto," and "morte" – suggest, moreover, a temporal sequence: love leads to tears, which lead to death. I have attempted to reflect this scheme as closely as possible in the translation.

12 "And so not finding it": his heart not finding death in the fire.

31
That dazzling flame *whose radiance first made*

Fiammetta's radiance disorients the lover's soul and forces it to wander trembling, unable to communicate. The lover's desire compensates by revealing what the soul seeks to hide from the public. "Flame" here and elsewhere is Fiammetta's *senhal,* Occitan for signal, signalling or indicating a specific object. The term appears in sonnets 29–32, each time in the first verse, linking them thematically.

32
The great desire that the flame *of love*

This *rima* is a fragment of a sestina, a fixed verse form consisting of six stanzas of six verses each, usually followed by a three-line envoi.

33
That loving light whose splendour introduced

The sonnet plays on the oxymoronic nature of gazing at the beloved. To see her results in the loss of seeing her, hence the conflict of wanting to see her while needing not to look at her.

1 "That loving light": this light is the object of the verb "are unable to endure" (6), whose subject is "pupils."

5 "this one of her and that one of the lord": the "sparks" (2) leave a portrait of her and another of Love in his heart.

34
If locks of curly golden hair, blonde braids

The sonnet exploits the trope of cataloguing the physical and moral virtues of the beloved.

7 "keys": the keys, an image and concept of Biblical origin, symbolize the overwhelming power and control of the lord of Love, who locks and unlocks the chains of love that bind the lover. The metaphor is typical of stilnovist poetry.

35

I never could, however much I gazed

Boccaccio's love for Fiammetta, unlike Dante's for Beatrice, is an earthbound love, and unlike Beatrice, Fiammetta does not come from and later return to paradise. Boccaccio's concept of the love of woman retains nothing of the spiritualism of *the stil novo.* Boccaccio inverts Dante's concept, making Fiammetta his "paradise on Earth" (4).

9 "those stars": the lady's eyes.

12 "towards them": towards her eyes.

36

Whenever Love leads me where I see you

The sonnet interweaves the themes of the luminous light emanating from the beloved's eyes, the oxymoronic nature of its effect on the lover, and the lover's sense of loss owing to the beloved's departure (14).

37

Bright pristine oriental pearls beneath

A cameo portrait of Fiammetta, and a gem of imagistic and stylistic beauty whose syntactical parts flow seamlessly, in praise of the lady's physical and moral qualities, employing the conventional metaphors of white teeth, ruby red lips, black brows, and golden yellow hair.

4 The planets of Jove and Venus, or stars, as Boccaccio would call them, represent Fiammetta's eyes.

14 "she bears the likeness of true angels": despite her likeness, Boccaccio's beloved lacks theological underpinnings, which separate her from Dante's Beatrice and the *stil novo.*

38

That pleasant song with which once Orpheus

The sonnet exalts Fiammetta's superhuman qualities, which no song or words could ever adequately portray.

2 Cerberus is the guardian of the underworld who allowed no one to return to earth. Orpheus succeeded in lulling him to sleep in his failed attempt to bring his beloved Eurydice back to life. Charon is the steersman who ferries dead souls across the Acheron and Styx rivers in the underworld.

3 Amphion is the king of Thebes who used magic to build the city's walls with his twin brother.

4 Dirce was a queen of Thebes.

5 "those who once adorned their brow / with laurel": the poets.

6 The Pegasian spring was on Mount Helicon.

13 "silent verses": verses unaccompanied by music.

39

Some say Partenope, the siren decked

The sonnet describes the foundation of Naples. It is a prelude to the next series of sonnets portraying the area of Baia on the Tyrrhenian coast.

1–3 Partenope was one of the sirens who tried to entice Ulysses, but, failing to succeed, she cast herself into the sea and drowned. Her body washed ashore at Naples ("in this area") on the island of Megaride, where the Castel dell'Ovo is now located.

7 "many treasured pages": the writings of classical authors.

12 "my lovely enemy": his beloved Fiammetta.

40

From time to time my soul will say to me

This and the nine sonnets that follow comprise a cycle featuring Baia, a popular summer resort area along the seashore directly south of Pozzuoli on the Gulf of Naples, where Fiammetta often vacationed. For Boccaccio, it is a site of moral laxity.

3 Bacchus is the Roman god of wine.

4 Ceres is the goddess of agriculture in Roman mythology. Both she and Bacchus epitomize excessive consumption.

41

One looking forward with delight to flowers

Boccaccio describes the beauty of Baia, which Fiammetta visits frequently in fair weather – a beauty that contrasts strongly with his painful feelings of rejection.

42

Avernus lies between the mountain peak

1 Avernus refers to either the lake or the general area southwest of Pozzuoli.

2 Mount Barbaro is the southern peak of Mount Gauro.

4 Misenum is the cape of the peninsula.

43

At times Zephyrus blows against my face

Lanza considers this the finest and most original *rima* of the Baia sequence (Lanza, *Le Rime*, 84).

4 The wind's escape from Ulysses's wineskins is recounted in book 10 of Homer's *Odyssey*, but Boccaccio learned of it from Ovid's *Metamorphoses* (14.223 ff).

8 An echo of Dante's image of Beatrice as a cloud: "li angeli che tornavan suso in cielo, / e una nuvoletta avean davanti" (angels soaring to their heavenly home[,] / and there before them rose ... a little cloud; *Vita nova* 23.59–60); and "così dentro una nuvola di fiori ... donn' m'apparve" (so in the bosom of a cloud of flowers ... a lady appeared; *Purg.* 30.28–32).

44

Caucasia, Cinto, Ida and Sigeum

The catalogue of mountains initiates a comparison in praise of Misenum, a promontory and town at the west end of the Gulf of Pozzuoli. Boccaccio also calls it a mountain in book 1 of his *De montibus*: "Misenus mons est campanus, Cumis proximus" (Mount Misenum is a rural mountain, next to Cumae; my translation).

8 Abyla in Africa and Calpe in Spain are the famous Pillars of Hercules.

45

Misenum, he from whom you took your name

Misenus, a companion of Aeneas who gave his name to the town where he was born, was drowned by Triton for his hubris in having challenged the gods to a musical contest (Verg. *Aen.* 6). The poet's "lord and king" (14), of course, is the god of love.

46

If I'm upset by Baia's sky and sea

A *contemptus Baiae* in which Boccaccio denounces the salacious character of the seaside resort.

2 The two "lakes" are the Avernus and the Lucrinus.

9–11 The conceit is that Venus, symbolizing lust, turns chaste women (Lucrece) into sensualists (Cleopatra).

47

May your name perish, Baia, with your town

Like the previous sonnet, a *vituperium* condemning Baia for having corrupted the morals of Fiammetta.

48

The falling snow and showers have now ceased

With the arrival of the "new season" (8), springtime, a time of love and festivity, the poet fears Fiammetta will return to Baia.

49

Most certainly when the fair sky regards

This concluding sonnet of the Baia cycle celebrates the annual renewal of its hedonistic rituals, although Boccaccio forgoes his customary critique of it, unlike in the previous sonnets.

5 "senz'alcun sospetto": the very words the lustful sinner Francesca speaks to the pilgrim Dante in the second circle of Hell (*Inf.* 5.129).

7–8 An allusion to the myth of the birth of Venus at sea.

50

Who would not very easily believe

The myth of Arion, cited from Ovid's *Fasti* (2.95 ff), serves as the sonnet's theme.

51

My lady sat accompanied by friends

The image of the lady sailing with friends recalls Dante's sailing fantasy in the sonnet "Guido, i' vorrei che tu e Lapo ed io" (Guido, I wish that Lapo, you, and I). See Dante Alighieri, *Dante's Lyric Poetry: Poems of Youth and of the* Vita Nuova, ed. Teodolinda Barolini, trans. Richard Lansing (Toronto: University of Toronto Press, 2014), 274–5.

8–11 These verses contain a clear echo of Dante's description of Beatrice's angelic nature in lines 7–8 of the sonnet "Tanto gentile e tanto onesta pare" (My lady shows such grace and dignity): "credo che sia una cosa venuta / da cielo in terra a miracol mostrare" (and I believe she is a creature come / from heaven to earth to show a miracle; Alighieri, *Dante's Lyric Poetry*, 280–1).

52

Love guided me, the sun still blazing hot

Another sailing scene, this time with the poet on board, introducing an idyllic setting in which his lady is heard singing with her friends.

2 The Julian gulf refers to the Gulf of Pozzuoli.

12 Lanza suggests that the image of the lady singing in a forest grove recalls Dante's Matelda in the closing cantos of the *Purgatorio* (Lanza, *Le Rime*, 105).

53

The Crab was blazing hot, the sext now past

The marine image again informs a scene of tranquility in which four sea gods gaze on the poet's lady in wonderment, along with the poet dazed by her beauty. The word "adoppiati" (benumbed) in verse 13 derives from *oppio*, the word for opium.

1 "The Crab was blazing hot": the sun was blazing strongly beneath the sign of the Crab in the zodiac.

5 "I saw the one": the poet's beloved, Fiammetta.

9 Neptune, Glaucus, Phorcys, and Tethys are sea gods. Glaucus was born a mortal and became a god; Phorcys (also Phorcus) was a primordial sea god who fathered the Gorgons; and Tethys, the wife of Oceanus, was the goddess of fresh water and mother of the river gods.

54

Barefoot, scantly dressed, her hair in braids

Many consider this sonnet Boccaccio's finest lyric composition for the natural simplicity of the seashore scene, its evocation of the lady's sensuality, and the small drama of the poet's role as onlooker, a motif continued from the previous *rima*. The poet-onlooker's slightly salacious gaze, unique in the *Rime*, is more characteristic of the world of the *Decameron*.

55

O happy day, O sky serene and bright

The sonnet relies on several rhetorical devices – anaphora, repetitio, exclamatio – in presenting an image of extraordinary beauty and felt wonder that is suddenly undermined in the last verse by one of violence, the onslaught of scores of arrows launched by Cupid. The word "mille" (14) expresses an indefinite number, not 1,000.

13 "secret power": the power of Cupid.

56

Her wavy golden hair tied back upon

The poet has a vision of his lady singing in a *locus amoenus*, an idyllic setting, a pleasant place.

10 "Love placed": Love placed the image of her hair, face, eyes, and bearing in the lover's mind. "Love" is the subject of the clause, "placed" the main verb.

13–14 Lifting his head, the lover sees his lady's beauty encircling it, his mind having been captured ("seized") by the lady's splendours ("they gave it to him") – that is, the splendours (enumerated in verses 1–8) gave his mind to Cupid. In other words, the fantasy becomes a reality.

57

Beside a spring, upon a narrow lea

The lyric dramatizes a scene of three ladies engaged in discussing their love affairs.

8 "two colours": the gold of the ladies' hair and the green of the foliage.

14 The word "ventura" here means good fortune, whereas in its previous use in verse 10, "per aventura," it has a neutral sense, meaning simply "by chance."

58

Beneath the shade of countless leafy trees

The lover, unaware, falls victim to the beauty of the lush setting and the conniving of a lovely little angel sowing hidden traps at the behest of Cupid.

59

I don't believe the sound that made the eyes

The lyric opens with an epic simile comparing three classical instances of soft sounds to the soft voice of a little angel. It introduces two different orders or worlds of experience, the mythological and the intimate, the effect of which is somewhat jarring.

2 Argus is the all-seeing giant of many eyes, epitomizing ideal vigilance.

3 Amphion is a son of Zeus and a renowned musician.

6 The Greek hero Ulysses was enchanted by the Sirens, whose sweet singing interrupted his homeward journey.

60

At times the sun ascending in the east

A sonnet structured on the principle of reversal, initiated by the adversative "but" (9). The sestet overturns the octave, as it were. The light of the sun, moon, and stars may be obscured on occasion, but not the light of Fiammetta's two eyes. The presence of the lady's *senhal*, "fiammette" (little flames), confirms that the sonnet is the work of Boccaccio.

61

The sea serene, the soil producing flowers

This sonnet relies on the catalogue topos and deploys a bipartite structure that presents images of peace and tranquility followed by a portrayal of the poet's emotional state. But the catalogue runs eleven verses before the adversative "but" appears, leaving just three verses to express the poet's opposite state of unease and discomfort. The feeling of sudden reversal produced in those three brief verses magnifies the reader's sense of the lover's suffering.

4 Aeolus is the divine ruler of the winds, Zephyrus the god of the west wind.

62

Who'd ever think some hidden ice could find

The *rima* plays on a series of oxymorons, the opposites fire and ice, hot and cold. The strange power of coldness sets the poet on fire with love, while the beloved, though likewise affected by it, remains chilly to his feelings for her.

63

As at the well Narcissus was possessed

This eleven-verse lyric is a madrigal, a popular short-verse form with a pastoral setting. It expresses an analogy between Narcissus and Fiammetta, exploiting the idea of self-love. Boccaccio imitates stylistically the effect of the mirrored or "imitated" self in the phrases "di sé da sé" (2), "sé, sé" (3), "vaga … vagheggia" (4), and "sé a sé" (7).

3 "she": the poet's lady.

14 In Greek mythology, Daphne, a nymph who rejected all suitors, escaped the embraces of the god Phoebus by being transformed into a tree. Ovid's account (*Met.* 1.438–567) is the most well known.

64
The other day my ardour carried me

The nymph (6), who approaches the poet and beckons him to follow her, is the figure of Poetry, who has the power to make the poet's name eternal. In his reading of the poet's reaction, Lanza argues that he rises not to follow her but rather to partake of a love feast, putting off any desire to seek fame through poetry (Lanza, *Le Rime,* 128).

2 The mountain Helicon was the home of the Muses.

6 "the lady from Laconia": Helen of Troy. Helen was born in Sparta, the chief city in the region of Laconia, and was married to King Menelaus of Sparta before her abduction by Paris of Troy.

13 "hell": a metaphoric expression for adversity.

65
Above the crimson flowers and curls of gold

The lyric announces the death of Fiammetta in imagery that recalls the ascent to heaven of Dante's Beatrice as a little cloud in the *Vita nova,* Boccaccio's "nugoletta" (3) echoing Dante's "nebuletta" (*Vita nova* 23.7). And verse 8, "d'orïental zafir vestita e d'oro," echoes one of Dante's most beautiful verses in the *Purgatorio,* "Dolce color d'oriental zaffiro" (Sweet color of oriental sapphire; 1.13). Note that verses 1, 4, 5, and 8 contain the same rhyme word, "oro" (gold), as if to suggest that Fiammetta's death is framed in gold.

66
The rivers have become all glass, the cold

The sonnet, which takes for its inspiration Dante's canzone "Io son venuto al punto de la rota" (I've come now to the point upon the wheel), is built on an elaborate oxymoron, exemplified by the opposites Boreas, the Greek god of the cold north wind, storms, and winter, and Vulcan, the Roman god of fire. The poet desires water (13) to assuage his fiery passion.

67
The legend has survived into our time

Zeus punishes Prometheus for having stolen fire from the gods by chaining him to a rock where the "hard beak" (4) of an eagle consumes his heart and liver daily. Being a god, Prometheus's organs would regenerate overnight and the following day be again consumed by the eagle in an endless cycle of punishment.

8 "composed it with my tears as pen and ink": the conceit is a literary topos – one that also appears in Cavalcanti's sonnet "Noi siàn le triste penne isbigotite" (We are the sad and disconcerted quills). See Guido Cavalcanti, *Rime*, vol. 2 of *Poeti del Duecento*, ed. Gianfranco Contini (Milan: Ricciardi, 1960).

12–14 The lover's fate replicates that of Prometheus.

68
Behind the shepherd of Admetus was

The theme of this sonnet, which has sixteen lines and is called a *sonetto ritornellato*, expresses the love for a widow.

1 "the shepherd of Admetus": Apollo, god of the sun.

2 "the one": Jove, who, taking the form of a bull, abducted Europa, the daughter of King Agenor of Phoenicia, a story depicted on the walls of Troy. The convoluted references signify that the time of year is mid-April through May, when the constellation of Taurus sets behind the sun.

5 "a woman, like the one": like Judith of Israel, who seduced and slew Holofernes, an Assyrian general.

8 "third of the eternal spheres": the planet Venus.

10 "the daughter of King Belus": Dido of Carthage.

13 "Byblis": the daughter of Miletus, who agonizes over her love for her twin brother Caunus. The poet burns with love for his lady and feels the ice of its paralyzing force.

69
Like one who's happy thinking about love

The poem, a *ternario* (a stanza of three lines), takes the form of a *sirventes* (an Occitan service song). Twelve young maidens (17), among whom Fiammetta appears (40), joined by Cupid and the lover, are identified. For a discussion of this poem, see Filosa, *Boccaccio's Florence*, 27–32.

53 "as she is aptly named by one you know": by Dante, who calls Giovanna, Cavalcanti's lady, "Primavera" in the *Vita nova* (15.9).

70
Sir Love, dear lord of ours

The song, a ballad, is closely tied to the previous lyric. It is a prayer to Cupid, the god of love. The ladies plead for Love's assistance in guiding them to love properly and protecting them by tempering the behaviour of male lovers.

28 "before we change our place": before they die and go to heaven.

45 "before he cruelly brings about our death": Cupid must bring them love or else they will die. The absence of love is a matter of life and death.

71

No longer do I dare lift up my eyes

This lyric, also a ballad, treats the theme of jealousy.

72

I don't know what I want

A short ballad that expresses the lover's ambivalence about the merits of desiring love versus death.

73

The flower that's lost its strength

A ballad in which a lady expresses her regret for having wasted her youth.

20 "until the fire of my life expires": the literal sense of the Italian, "fintanto / che 'l foco di mia vita giugna al verde," means to live until the fire of the speaker's life "reaches the green." The metaphor derives from the image of a candle whose base is made of green wax and whose wick burns down until it reaches the base, where it burns out.

74

The painful hunger, the Tyrrhenian depths

A list of the many ways by which the unhappy lover considers committing suicide. The last verse suggests he lacks the courage to follow through.

13 "the many ways": that is, "brutal ways to die" (8).

14 "but then he won't risk his unhappy life": "he" refers back to "like one" (13), but it means the poet himself. In the end, he lacks the courage to take his own life.

75

Hippocrates, Avicenna, or Galen

13 "and it drives": the "excruciating spirit of love" (10) drives away all other griefs.

76

Gryphons, wolves, lions, serpents, snakes

Another sonnet that relies on the catalogue motif as a figure of *amplificatio.*

9–11 "But I, not being like that": that is, since the poet is not like that, why does his beloved flee from him as if he were someone to be dreaded, then not return until she sees that he has gone away? The verses highlight the ironic, almost comic interplay of the lady's fleeing and then the lover's need to flee.

13 "If I were wearing horns": Satan is depicted in popular culture as having horns on his head.

77

Why go on testing me in vain, lord Love

The lover boasts that Love has failed to recapture him now that he is old.

78

My foolish mind has so completely gone

Desire for the love object is irrational and destroys even the lover's attempts at penitence. The convoluted syntax and multiple, intertwined dependent clauses express a sense of turmoil and restlessness that reflect the lover's loss of emotional stability and his unrestrainable rush, "smarrito / corro" (7–8), towards death.

79

Unwise is he who thinks that he can change

A spirit of misogyny underlies the lover's criticism of the evils of women in this *rima*.

5–6 It was a popular belief that making sounds could help the moon move through the heavens.

80a

Two lovely ladies Love will often bring

Boccaccio opens a debate, a *tenzone*, regarding whether one should prefer the love of a young woman or that of a widow, inviting responses from other poets. A *sonetto rintornellato* of sixteen lines, this *rima* inaugurates a series of nine successive sonnets in the same form. The incipit is modelled on Dante's *Rime* 84, in which the two ladies in question are Beauty and Virtue. Antonio Pucci (c. 1310–88) was a Florentine self-taught versifier. His response to Boccaccio will be followed by Riccio's sonnet addressed to Boccaccio, who then replies with one of his own.

80b

You've come so forcefully into my heart

Pucci advises Boccaccio to choose the widow over the virgin as his lady. The lily, "giglio" (16), symbolizes purity and chastity.

81a

If I spoke better than Carmenta did

Riccio initiates a *tenzone* with Boccaccio that asks two questions about the relationship between love and the woman loved.

1 Carmenta was the goddess of childbirth and prophecy in Roman mythology. Her name derives from the Latin word *carmen*, meaning magic spell or oracle, and also song. It is the root of the English word "charm" and also the name Carmen.

3 "the sun would find itself in Orion": since Orion is not a constellation of the Zodiac, the sun cannot occupy its house for a period of the year on a regular basis.

81b

When the realm of Ethiopia

Boccaccio replies to Riccio that his view is wrongly conceived because love derives from astral influence, which imposes specific dispositions on individuals (see Branca, *Rime*, 262).

2 Rhodopes is a mountain range in Trace, in northern Greece and southern Bulgaria.

4 "noble essence": the constellation of Taurus, "ascending" when the planet Venus is in its house.

5 "la Sidonïa": Dido, who was originally from Sidonia, a town in Phoenicia, and who was receptive to the influence of Venus.

10 Boccaccio uses a metaphor to express how he makes a good argument: "con quale ago vedrai punga la mosca," literally translated, is "you'll see with which needle I prick your fly."

82a

Let heaven, even heaven, heed the law

Ser Cecco initiates a *tenzone* espousing the view that humans cannot know what their Maker wills (12–14) and that the stars do not determine human acts. Francesco di Miletto de Rossi worked as chancellor of Francesco Ordelaffi, lord of Forlì, together with Nereo Morandi.

2 "vast wheels": the nine heavens of the Ptolemaic system.

4 "'l centro inscritto": "the inscribed centre" is the Earth, the centre of the universe. I have translated the meaning rather than the language of the words.

8 “lunar cloudiness”: solar eclipses by the moon.

10 “poisoned shafts”: that is, disease or contagion.

14 “to offer signs”: to warn of impending misfortune.

82b
Since the eternal motion spoken of

Petrarch’s response follows suit in rejecting the notion of astral influence.

4 “the great theorist of Egypt”: the Greek astrologer Ptolemy, who lived in Alexandria.

7 “Phoebus”: Apollo, the Sun.

8 “his sister’s motion counter to his course”: the Moon when moving counter to the Sun can produce eclipses.

9–13 “no one ... is able to denote how much our life / can be expected to be safe and firm”: that is, no one, without God’s consent, can see the future.

16 “the path a star takes”: the star’s movement can’t harm it, that is, have an effect on “it,” namely, the world.

82c
Let every man who wears attire required

Humans through the use of free will determine whether actions or events can be said to be good or evil. Lancillotto Anguissola was a friend of Petrarch’s who lived in Piacenza.

8 “once in Egypt”: when God persecuted the Egyptians who were oppressing the Israelites (Exodus 7–12).

82d
Heaven, and its firmament, is fixed

The implication is that because the stars are close to the divine, humans tend to attribute to them their inadequacies, thereby giving encouragement to the theory of astral influence, which the poet believes is false. Antonio Beccari da Ferrara was a major poet in the court of the Ordelaffi in the years 1347–8.

6 “jewels”: the stars.

8 “passïone”: “torment,” that is, destruction.

82e

The ancient father whose initial crime

1 "ancient father": Adam, whose "initial crime" was the first, and hence original, sin.

4 "created then": Adam was born in Eden, the perfect world of happiness and innocence, but he did not on that account moderate his desires.

5 "rebellious people": the Israelites, who failed to follow "counsel that was right" (8), namely, the will of God.

6 "their ordeals": the ten plagues (Exodus 7–12).

9–11 Humans are not troubled by the distance in time between them and Adam and Eve, who had greater proximity to God; following God's will is less "burdensome for perfect souls," that is, for those who are perfect.

12–13 "clouds / being ruptured": thunder.

15 "The one who died to end our servitude": Christ, who redeemed mankind from the bondage of sin.

82f

When Julius Caesar was prevented from

Ser Cecco asserts that the heavens presage future conflict with clear signs. Such power of nature, directed by Providence, should instill fear in humans that only arrogance can dismiss.

1 Caesar was denied entry into Rome by the Senate in 50 BCE.

7–8 "a veil / of black": the eclipse of the sun.

10 "the moment Brutus drew his knife": the assassination of Caesar in 44 BCE.

83a

The heavens and the gods, the age and Fortune

Hannibal's address to Scipio just before the Battle of Zama in 202 BCE. The poem is a *strambotto,* a single-stanza verse form of eight hendecasyllabic lines, among the earliest forms in medieval Italian poetry. Boccaccio's text for the tenzone is taken from the third decade of Livio's *Ab urbe condita* (30.30–31).

8 "the dark way": the difficult way (i.e., war).

83b
Hannibal, the peace accords you broke

Scipio's bold reply to Hannibal, claiming victory over his forces.

2 "Sagunto": a Spanish city attacked by Hannibal in 219 BCE.

7 "such is the gain": the phrase is ironic.

84
As many times as I pass by the place

This and the following sonnet are paired, treating the same experience of recalling the first moments of Boccaccio and Fiammetta falling in love, his in the present *rima,* then hers in the next. The two sonnets share several identical rhyme words: "foco" (84.4, 85.13), "poco" (84.5, 85.10), "acceso" / "accesa" (84.13, 85.1), and "difeso" / "difesa" (84.7, 85.4). This linguistic interplay suggests that the two lovers' feelings are still, in some sense, intertwined.

85
Love draws me to the place where I was first

The speaker is the poet's mistress, Fiammetta, who recalls the time and place she fell in love with him.

1 "the place": most likely the church of San Lorenzo in Naples.

14 My translation follows Branca's reading, but "and I look back at him" might be rendered to suggest that the beloved, whose sight of her lover has revived her love, has been reconciled with herself, returning her to her previous self.

86
Were I, lord Love, to see you even once

The poet's rebuke of Cupid for striking him with arrows but not his mistress is a topos in lyric poetry.

5 "daring": the word "baldanzosa" clearly echoes Dante's description of Lisetta in *Rime* 117.3, linking Fiammetta with her (though not with Beatrice who, as the ideal woman, has no place in Boccaccio's poetry).

87
You've found me, Love, defenseless and alone

The poet continues his attack on Cupid for unjustly making him a victim and taking pleasure in it. The motif of the defenseless lover lacking armour to ward off Cupid's arrows finds an echo in Petrarch's *Canzoniere* 3.

88

What are you doing, trying to do, by filing

Cupid answers the protests that the poet addressed to him in the previous sonnet.

89

If Zephyr has by now not pacified

The poet hopes that the power of the wind will placate Fiammetta's cruelty and cause her to take pity on his suffering.

1 "non disacerba": words echoing Petrarch's *Canzoniere* 23.4 and 190.8, just as Zephyr echoes the Petrarchan "Zefiro torna" in sonnet 310.1.

90

The high hope that once used to mitigate

The motif of the lady having grown grey and wrinkled with the passage of time is topical in classical as well as medieval literature. Boccaccio employs here the same rhymes – "desiri" / "sospiri" / "martirî" – as Dante does in his portrayal of Francesca in *Inferno* 5.116 ff.

8 This verse is missing in the manuscript on which Lanza relies. It is the only manuscript that contains this sonnet. Lanza supplies a possible reading, which I have placed between angle brackets.

91

If it should ever happen that my years

The poet delights in seeing Fiammetta lose her beauty with age, which he views as just punishment for her "former stinginess" (14) in granting him any pleasure.

3 "turn silvery": the original colour "argento," silver, plays against the colour of gold, suggesting a decline to a less ideal form of life.

13 "no longer count": no longer find appeal in public.

92

As often as I reminisce about

The poet reflects on his sense of being a victim of love, which enrages him to the point that he curses the day he fell in love, leading him to seek out death as a way of ending his suffering.

1 Boccaccio uses the same opening verse in sonnet 116, which shows an indebtedness to Petrarch's *Canzoniere* 281.1.

93

You have surpassed the high point of your years

The poet's soul invokes him to reject love and turn his mind to spiritual matters as he grows old. But the poet is unable to accept such advice upon once again seeing Fiammetta, who causes him to fold his wings and follow her.

12 "then to the lofty flight it rests its wings": the soul ceases thinking about salvation.

94

If I, Love, see the day when you release

The poet looks to the day when he can escape the bonds of Love and assert that he will never return to such a state of servitude.

8 "consuming grass up in the alpine peaks": like a beast in the wilderness.

12–13 "and made of me a laughing stock before / the tiresome crowd": echoes lines from Petrarch's *Canzoniere* 1.9–10: "Ma ben veggio or sì come al popol tutto / favola fui gran tempo" (But I now see quite well how I for a long time was the talk of the crowd). All English translations of Petrarch's *Canzoniere* are taken from Francesco Petrarca, *Petrarch's Lyric Poems: The* Rime sparse *and Other Lyrics,* ed. and trans. Robert M. Durling (Cambridge, MA: Harvard University Press, 1976).

95

When I look at myself, by far more fragile

The image of Fiammetta inscribed in the poet's mind continues to inspire his love for her, which will last until death, despite his having wasted his time loving her in the past. The motif of the inscribed image of the beloved is a topos of medieval literature. The first to use it in vernacular Italian literature was Giacomo da Lentini, in the famous *canzonetta* "Meravigliosa-mente" (Extraordinarily): "che 'nfra o core mio / porto la tua figura" (for in my heart I bear / the image of your form). See Giacomo da Lentini, *The Complete Poetry of Giacomo da Lentini,* trans. Richard Lansing (Toronto: University of Toronto, 2018), 25.

2 "glass": Boccaccio alludes to his patron Niccolò Acciaiuoli's criticism of him as being so sensitive as to be as fragile as glass ("uomo di vetro"). The poet had once departed abruptly while visiting him, having found his patron's generosity wanting.

96

If Love, whose conduct you for many years

The poet-lover meditates on his present state, chastising himself for wanting, even in old age, to cling to his amorous desires and imploring himself to accept and take pity on his new condition.

97

Your quick and clever wit had lost its strength

Fiammetta, taking on the role of muse in the poet's mind, prompts her lover to recall how she inspired him to seek praise for his poetry, exhorting him to persevere in his quest. Some critics assign the voice to Poetry writ large, and while either reading is defensible, Boccaccio is less likely to be thinking abstractly than about himself here.

11 "crown of leaves": the laurel wreath symbolizes the highest achievement in a competition, in this case in the sphere of poetry.

98

From time to time as I look at the sun

This and the following eight sonnets explore the theme of the lady's death, in imitation of Petrarch's lyrics of Laura *in morte*. Fiammetta's close association with the sun is highlighted by the repetition of the word "sole" in the first and fourth rhyme positions of the two ABBA quatrains.

4 "my burning sun": Fiammetta.

99

Asleep one day, within a dream I seemed

Boccaccio dreams of ascending towards heaven following behind Fiammetta, but suddenly he awakes and is brought back to reality. Lanza notes that the model for this sonnet is Petrarch's *Canzoniere* 302 (Lanza, *Le Rime*, 216).

100

If the flame *of her eyes, now sanctified*

The poet imagines that the sight of Fiammetta's eyes might draw him closer to God, but then he realizes that she "disdains / all mortal things" (9–10), including him, and that any moral ascent seems unlikely.

6 "highest Good": God.

11 "drive me where I burn the most": towards heaven and Fiammetta (see Lanza, *Le Rime*, 219).

101
Still searching, fool? Still looking everywhere?

In an apparition, Fiammetta implores Boccaccio to turn to God, who manages only to give thought to such an act. Branca observes that Fiammetta's words to the poet recall Dante's presentation of Beatrice in the final cantos of Dante's *Purgatorio* (Branca, *Rime*, 282).

102
Dante, if you dwell in the sphere of love

Boccaccio beseeches Dante, who he imagines resides among the saved, to implore Fiammetta to bring about a return to her after his death.

1 "the sphere of love": the heaven of Venus, the third sphere.

3 "Bice": the shortened form of Beatrice's name.

8 "by thinking": the souls in heaven do not need to speak since they communicate by means of contemplation through looking at each other.

12 In classical mythology, the underworld river Lethe had the power of causing memory loss in those who drank its waters.

103
The sky was clear and calm, adorned with stars

In a nocturnal setting the poet sees streaking across the sky the flame of Fiammetta, who warns the poet that entry into paradise requires the acquisition of virtue on his part.

11–12 Fiammetta enumerates the qualities of character required of the poet-lover for her to accept his love. They are commonplace in stilnovist poetry, but in this instance Boccaccio inverts a metaphor, playing on a well-known verse from Dante's *Vita nova* 17.6, where Beatrice is described as "d'umiltà vestita" (dressed in humbleness). Here it is he, the lover, not the beloved, who is so dressed, as Kumar pointedly emphasizes in his introduction above.

104
The lyrics that my youthful voice once made

Boccaccio regrets losing his ability to write poetry after the death of Fiammetta. The sonnet is modelled on Petrarch's *Canzoniere* 293.

7 The Italian term “specchi” means “mirrors,” which is a common metaphor for the eyes, suggesting that one’s eyes can reflect the soul or the thoughts and emotions of a person.

11 “another’s loveliness”: the beauty of God.

105 *Homer’s divine creativity*

Since artists of the past have failed to describe female beauty adequately, Boccaccio feels immune to self-criticism on that account.

3 “Zeuxis”: the most celebrated Greek painter of antiquity. To paint the image of Helen of Troy, he chose to depict the most beautiful parts of five models in order to create her perfect form. The account is narrated by Cicero (*De inventione* 1.2).

6–7 “the glorious good / of paradise”: Fiammetta.

106
So strong and so intense is my desire

This sonnet is clearly based on Dante’s sonnet “Oltre la spera” (Beyond the sphere), the final poem of the *Vita nova*, and on Petrarch’s *Canzoniere* 302, “Levommi il mio penser” (My thought lifted me up), each recounting a journey to a beloved now deceased.

13 “when my spirits, which only seek for peace”: only after the poet returns to his senses will he be able to write about Fiammetta’s beauty.

14 “the place where they belong”: as his spirits were before his fantasy, in their normal place.

107
O Justice, queen who keeps the world in check

The lyric, a madrigal, has two stanzas of three verses with the rhyme pattern ABB CDD, followed by a rhyming couplet EE.

2 “by the highest heaven’s lofty power”: by Providence, in the Empyrean.

108
All virtue’s fled, what is of value dead

The poet laments the universal loss of virtue owing to greed and a diminished commitment to values espoused by literature.

3 “the Castalian Muses”: the Muses reside on Mount Parnassus, at the spring of Castalia.

5 “verde lauro”: the laurel crown, symbolizing poetry.

13 "l'uso moderno": the "modern ways" recalls *Purgatorio* 16.42, "modo tutto fuor del moderno uso" (in a manner completely outside of modern usage).

109

Apicius and Sardanapalus

A denunciation of Avarice, one of the seven capital sins.

1 Apicius, author of *De re coquinaria* (On cooking), a Roman gourmet celebrated for his gluttony, lived during the reign of Tiberius. Sardanapalus, legendary king of Assyria, was well known for his depravity.

110

Long and hard did Saturn study ways

Exempla of individuals famous for their achievements, cited as models of virtue in society. But today the learned are considered those who seek to acquire wealth, so that their learning consists in and is a form of wasting time.

3 "the servile arts": another term for the mechanical arts.

111

So much has everyone turned their sights to

Those who desire to acquire wealth are so numerous that other kinds of labour are deemed madness. Boccaccio beseeches Apollo (Phoebus) to reward him with the laurel crown for his dedication to poetry.

112

While hoping to cross over both the one

The twin peaks of Mount Parnassus – Cirrha, sacred to Apollo, and Nissa, sacred to the Muses – inspire Boccaccio to strive for the laurel crown ("fronds"; 4), but old age has sapped his energy and forced him to abandon his journey, leaving him at a loss about what to write.

3 The Castalian spring was regarded as a source of poetic inspiration by Roman poets, and hence linked to the Muses.

113

The living waters of Parnassus Spring

This sonnet, closely allied to the previous one, recounts the poet's loss of confidence in his creative powers.

1 "Parnassus Spring": another name for the Castalian Spring.

4 "lovely stars": the eyes of Fiammetta.

8 "my goal": "ad elle," to them, that is, to the fronds of verse 2, the crown of Apollo.

114

Awaiting death is something difficult

The fixed span of life is compensated by the exercise of one's expertise in the quest to achieve fame, which extends life beyond mortality.

115

So many times we've sailed out on the sea

The navigation metaphor of life as a ship under sail was a familiar and oft-used topos in medieval literature. Boccaccio now prepares to return to port and the end of life. The previous and successive lyrics adopt variations of the same theme of preparing for death.

10–11 Christ, metaphorically the stone upon which the Church is built, joins the two walls of the Temple of Solomon, which most likely symbolize the Old and New Testaments.

116

As often as I look back on the past

The poet, facing his mortality, grieves for having wasted his past in pursuing temporal delight and hopes redemption is nevertheless still possible.

6 "for feeling what is given to us all": time, which has hurried by for him and everyone else.

117

Time flies, and yet the woeful sufferer

Another sonnet whose theme is based on the topos *tempus fugit.* These late lyrics have a strong tone of moralism, and in this instance lassitude and lethargy form the central sin.

7 "talent wasted": the reference is general and may refer to the poet's virtue, fame, or salvation.

14 "fishes with no line": an idiom meaning to waste time.

118

The highest Good presents itself to us

God, "the highest Good," brings spiritual treasures to all, the offering of salvation. But those who backslide trade "eternal peace" (13) for "everlasting fire" (14). Boccaccio juxtaposes here the "temporal good" (11) with the spiritual good, earthly love with divine love.

119

Now turn yourself around, tired spirit, turn

The poet exhorts himself to seek redemption by returning to God. The sonnet has a directness, conciseness, and sense of urgency expressed by the repeated use of verbs in the imperative that raise it above the norm.

14 "the last hired hand": a reference to the parable in Matthew 20:1–16, in which the hired person receives the same salary as those previously hired.

120

O Sun, who shines on this and on the other

Boccaccio appeals to Christ, the "Sun," to assist him in repenting his past sins. Note the efficacious rhyming of "mondo" (world) with "pondo" (weight) and "fondo" (world below, the Earth). Sin is the weight of the world.

121

O glorious King, who governs heaven with

This sonnet continues the theme of the previous one, both taking the form of a prayer.

12 "mortal iciness": coldness of loving what's good, or acedia, one of the seven capital sins, meaning spiritual sloth or apathy.

122

No golden tress, no splendour of the eyes

The first of three sonnets dedicated to the Virgin Mary.

10 "age-old spite": the injury brought about by original sin.

12 "offer it to us": refers to "your humility" in verse 9.

123

O everlasting light, O morning star

The sonnet is based on the liturgical text of "Salve Regina."

1 "morning star": associated with the Virgin Mary; its appearance on the horizon announces the promise of salvation.

3–4 "The helm of Peter's ship," which is also "the wagon of / the biform gryphon," is the Church. The "plaustro" (wagon or plough) bears Mary, the mother of Christ, who, being both human and divine, is biform in nature.

The gryphon, a creature with the head of an eagle and the body of a lion, likewise symbolizes the double nature of Christ. The symbolic wagon and beast are taken from Dante and appear in the allegorical Procession in *Purgatorio* 32.96.

14 "blessed Fruit": Christ.

124
O Queen of all the angels, O Maria

This is the last of the three successive homages to the Virgin Mary.

1 "Queen of all the angels": taken from the litany "Regina angelorum."

6 "where you abide": in heaven.

10 "may my long love avail me": a direct citation of the familiar and oft-cited verse from Dante's *Inferno* 1.83: "vagliami 'l lungo studio e 'l grande amore" (may my long study and great love avail me).

125
You run me through, and I'm not made of steel

In this *vituperium*, Boccaccio rebukes one of his detractors who, according to Franco Suitner, accused him of immorality (Franco Suitner, "Le rime di Boccaccio," in *Dante, Petrarca e altra poesia antica* [Florence: Cadmo, 2005], 218). Lanza, on the other hand, argues that Boccaccio is referring to events described in the following lyric (Lanza, *Le Rime*, 264).

126
Since you have ridiculed me so severely

The infamous act of the unnamed priest is that at the age of fifty he fathered a child with his domestic servant and then committed infanticide by drowning it in a latrine.

14 "you baptized him": it should not escape the reader that one of the roles of a priest is to baptize newborn infants.

127
You have ascended now, my dearest lord

This poem is a lament on the death of Petrarch in July 1374. Boccaccio will die the following year.

1 "You have ascended now:" Petrarch's ascent into heaven.

6–7 The poet evokes the memory of Petrarch's Laura (Lauretta) together with his own Fiammetta. Both are placed in the rhyme position of consecutive verses 6 and 7 in the Italian text, as if to express their affiliation as deceased beloved ladies. Verse 8 ends with God, suggestive of the ladies' divinity, and verse 9 with Dante, as if to allude to yet another lady, his beloved Beatrice.

9–10 Petrarch wrote a lament on the death of Sennuccio, which Boccaccio here imitates. Cino da Pistoia was Boccaccio's law professor in Naples and a friend of Dante who wrote more than 200 canzoni and sonnets, exchanging some with Dante.

Poems of Uncertain Attribution

1
As soon as the sun hides itself from us

The end of day and encroaching night, which contrasts the pleasant nighttime rest of all beings with the poet-lover's distress, here his inability to sleep, is a classical literary topos. Boccaccio draws on Dante's *notturno* at the beginning of *Inferno* 2: "Lo giorno se n'andava, e l'aere bruno / toglieva li animai che sono in terra / da le fatiche loro" (The day was ending and the darkened sky / was setting free the living beings on earth / from their hard work; my translation).

5 "the Ganges": the river signifies the Orient in general, being the furthest point east (cf. Dante, *Par.* 2.3).

2
The rugged mountains and the yawning vales

The sonnet deploys the catalogue motif or topos, a long list of items or descriptive features. Here the landscape is cause for the traveller's joy, which upon returning home is turned to grief as he is met by a scornful wife. Branca believes this sonnet is more likely by Petrarch than by Boccaccio (Branca, *Rime,* 255).

3
The golden hair adorned with verdant fronds

Lanza strongly doubts that Boccaccio could have composed this sonnet, which contains an imperfect rhyme in verse 5, "atti" with "-ati" in verses 1, 4, and 8 (Lanza, *Le Rime,* 276).

4
Not meadows, gardens, lovely dances, songs

The two tercets following the two quatrains in the manuscripts clearly do not belong to this sonnet, hence Lanza omits them from his edition.

5

My will has many times gone to my heart

Both Lanza and Branca strongly doubt the paternity of Boccaccio for this sonnet (Lanza, *Le Rime*, 289; Branca, *Rime*, 306).

2 "to indicate to her": to Fiammetta.

6

My eyes have robbed my heart and placed it in

A series of topoi and personifications regarding the amatory experience. Lanza believes this sonnet has a good chance of being by Boccaccio (Lanza, *Le Rime*, 281).

7

I thought I had most certainly regained

The lover escapes captivity in Cupid's prison only to suffer being recaptured and returned to bondage. Lanza believes the sonnet is probably by Boccaccio (Lanza, *Le Rime*, 282).

8

I have worn out by now a thousand pens

The image of the lover wearing out pens writing about his suffering derives from Petrarch's *Canzoniere* 23.10–12: "ben che 'l mio duro scempio / sia scritto altrove, sì che mille penne / ne son già stanche" (although my harsh undoing / is written elsewhere so that a thousand pens / are already tired by it). Lanza thinks the poem is quite possibly by Boccaccio (Lanza, *Le Rime*, 284).

9

I had already put aside my tears

The sonnet relies on the typical theme of a reversal of fortune. The poet initially experiences hope in a moment of freedom from Cupid's assault, but his lady renews her scorn and returns him to a state of misery without answering his pleas for mercy.

10

I used to speak of love quite frequently

The death of his lady denies the poet any relief from suffering since the splendour of her image can never return to assuage his pain.

11

Whether Love or a resplendent star

A sonnet of the same theme and inspiration as in the previous poem. Lanza remarks that the poem is very likely by Boccaccio (Lanza, *Le Rime,* 290).

14 "be no longer deaf!": the lover addresses Death directly, imploring him to assist in ending his life.

12

The hidden spirits and the shade of fronds

This canzone with five stanzas of thirteen verses each, followed by an envoi, sings the praises of an unknown individual who benefits from favours granted by Venus, Mars, and Pallas. In a number of places the meaning of the text proves resistant to interpretation. Many references and constructions remain unclear (e.g., verses 17–19, 26, 34–6, 46–52, 55, 62–3).

1–3 Winter deprives trees of their vital spirits and the shade that their leaves provide.

5 "by such": by winter and its elements, the phenomena produced by winter.

33 "in whose heart that sign is sad": a possible reference to a previously rejected lover.

59 "her celebrated wealth": her beauty.

60 "long-standing lord": the "lord of love" (22), Cupid.

62–3 "and you bestowed the way / with many lovely hues": the sense seems to be, "you showed your approval of the transfer in many lovely different ways." Branca remarks that the meaning of the passage is very problematic (Branca, *Rime,* 329).

74 "the goddesses": Venus and Pallas, with Mars being excluded possibly because of his role as god of war.

13

Sweet Ave Maria, *who is full of grace*

Lanza deems this *rima* as mediocre and, if by Boccaccio, written in his early youth (Lanza, *Le Rime,* 302).

1 "*Ave Maria*": the Angelic Salutation to Mary. The text is "Hail Mary, full of grace, the Lord is with thee; blessed art thou amongst women, and blessed is the fruit of thy womb."

10 "the Sun": divine grace.

12 "three palms": a metaphor for the three elements required by the sacrament of penitence: contrition of the heart, confession of the mouth, and satisfaction through good deeds, which are spelled out in the following verses.

25–6 "wolf / with seven limbs": the wolf, symbolizing collectively the seven capital sins, is an image taken from Dante's *Commedia.*

42 "*Consummatum est*": "it is finished," the lasts words of Christ.

48 "eternal counsel": paradise.

54 "the light and dark in us": the virtues and the vices.

60 "a prophet": John the Baptist.

62–3 "blessed art thou amongst women, and blessed is the fruit of thy womb."

64–8 "Elizabeth with all my heart … and from where to me this … above all gifts."

93 "*Osanna*": Hosannah, which means "pray, save us."

113 "the lofty stairs": the stairway to paradise.

115 "white and blonde": the silver florin and the gold florin.

122 "'n *excelsis*": on high.

123 "*Miserere*": "Have mercy on me."

135 "the boat of death": the ferry of Charon, who transports the souls of the dead across the Acheron river in hell.

145 "the foxes of deceit": temptations.

147 "so that fire burns it up": so that the fire of damnation will destroy it (i.e., strip the soul of its flesh, its essence).

14
To say you're beautiful

An isolated stanza of a ballad. Branca rejects it as the work of Boccaccio, while Lanza is inclined to accept it (Branca, *Rime,* 345; Lanza, *Le Rime,* 308).

15
My flame *grows even as I gaze on it*

The flame, the poet's love, increases continually as he gazes on it, which in turn elevates his mind to worthy ends. The theme is a topos of stilnovist poetry.

16
Love, you who bring together hearts and souls

The usual topoi of love: two hearts in one, pain turned to pleasure, the oxymoron fire and ice, hardness ("diamonds") and softness ("assuage my spirit"). The sonnet's two terzinas are missing.

17
As long as it feels power from your fair eyes

The light issuing from the eyes of the beloved ennoble the lover, but it is so great – "a burning sun!" (14) – that it blinds the lover. The divinity of the lady, it seems to suggest, is beyond the comprehension of the lover.

12 "divinity": the divine sun-lady.

18
Oh, how wonderful

An isolated stanza of a ballad. On the basis of linguistic incompatibility, Lanza excludes it from Boccaccio's *rime* (Lanza, *Le Rime*, 313).

19
My dearest brothers, behold the morose

A typical moralistic *memento mori* in the realistic popular vein. The poem is unlike any other by Boccaccio's hand, if it is by Boccaccio, which Lanza doubts (Lanza, *Le Rime*, 314).

13–14 No manuscript contains these two verses, and while Lanza supplies his own possible reading, I have left the lacuna in place, preferring not to make the *rima* more *dubbia* than it already is.

Poems of Boccaccio's Response to His Adversaries

In four lyrics Boccaccio expresses his rejection of criticism levelled at him for having agreed to the request of the municipal government of Florence to deliver a series of lectures on Dante and readings of the *Commedia* to the general public, events that took place in late 1373. Despite Lanza's disavowal of their authenticity and whether or not they are or in fact can be said to be authentic, they have found a place in critical discussions of Boccaccio's lyrics and in the cultural legacy he passed on to posterity. While Lanza lists these poems in an appendix among those he labels *rime spurie* (spurious lyrics), I have included them here to give readers the opportunity to judge for themselves how best to assess their significance, as well as to provide access to an understanding of their meaning.

1
If I have basely vilified the Muses

This and the following three lyrics are widely believed to refer to Boccaccio's reading of and lecturing about Dante's *Commedia* to the general public of Florence. The undertaking of the project, authorized by the government, took place over the course of several months from late October of 1373 through the beginning of 1374. The identity of the detractor Boccaccio seeks to appease is unknown.

2
If Dante grieves, wherever he may be

The poet expresses regret for undertaking his readings of Dante to the public in Florence, which he now calls a "[v]ain hope" (9) and which was brought about as well by constrained economical circumstances (8).

2 "lofty intellect": Dante invokes his own genius with the phrase "alto ingegno" in *Inferno* 2.7.

10 "judgment of my friends": the encouragement of those who solicited the municipal government to have Boccaccio deliver lectures on Dante's poetry to the masses.

3
They've more or less demeaned and wearied me

2 "your verses": those of Boccaccio's detractors, the same critics he refers to in the previous lyric ("as you have said"; 2.4).

3 "scratch the itch": a phrase taken from Dante's *Paradiso* 17.129, where Cacciaguida denounces Dante's enemies.

5 "them": the "verses" of line 2.

6 "penna": a metaphor for literary style, with the implication that his detractors lacked the skill and the culture of writers in Bologna.

10 "what has foolishly been said and done": the folly of disseminating Dante to the general, illiterate public.

4
I've put the thankless rabble in a ship

1 "thankless rabble": presumably the "ungrateful artisans" described in the second *rima*, verse 12.

1 "in a ship": the navigation imagery recalls Dante's *Paradiso* 2.1–9, but it is a basic topos in medieval literature.

7 "they": his detractors.

9 "lofty place": the poet imagines himself, in the nautical metaphor, to be sitting at the top of the ship's mainmast.

13 "the laurel": the laurel wreath or crown, for Boccaccio the award for the highest achievement among poets.

Bibliography

Editions of Boccaccio's *Rime*

Boni, Giovanni Battista Baldelli, ed. *Rime di Messer Giovanni Boccacci.* Livorno: Tommaso Masi & Co., 1802.

Branca, Vittore, ed. *Rime.* By Giovanni Boccaccio. Vol. 5.1 of *Tutte le opere di Giovanni Boccaccio.* Milan: Mondadori, 1992.

Lanza, Antonio, ed. *Le Rime.* By Giovanni Boccaccio. Rome: Aracne, 2010.

Leporatti, Roberto, ed. *Rime.* By Giovanni Boccaccio. Florence: SISMEL Edizioni del Galluzzo, 2013.

Massera, Aldo Francesco, ed. *La Caccia di Diana e Le Rime.* By Giovanni Boccaccio. Turin: UTET, 1914.

Other Primary Works Cited

Alighieri, Dante. *Dante's Lyric Poetry: Poems of Youth and of the* Vita Nuova. Edited by Teodolinda Barolini. Translated by Richard Lansing. Toronto: University of Toronto Press, 2014.

Alighieri, Dante. *The Divine Comedy.* Edited by Charles S. Singleton. 3 vols. Princeton, NJ: Princeton University Press, 1970–5.

Alighieri, Dante. *Rime.* Vol. 3 of *Testi,* edited by Domenico De Robertis. Florence: Le Lettere, 2002.

Alighieri, Dante. *Vita nova.* Edited by Guglielmo Gorni. Turin: Einaudi, 1996.

Alighieri, Dante. *Vita Nuova.* Translated by Virginia Jewiss. New York: Penguin, 2022.

Boccaccio, Giovanni. *Decameron.* Edited by Vittore Branca. 2 vols. Turin: Einaudi, 2004.

Boccaccio, Giovanni. *The Decameron.* Translated by Wayne A. Rebhorn. New York: Norton, 2013.

Boccaccio, Giovanni. *De montibus.* Edited by M. Pastore Stocchi. Vol. 8 of *Tutte le opere di Giovanni Boccaccio,* edited by Vittore Branca. Milan: Mondadori, 1998.

Cavalcanti, Guido. *Rime.* Vol. 2 of *Poeti del Duecento,* edited by Gianfranco Contini. Milan: Ricciardi, 1960.

Giacomo da Lentini. *The Complete Poetry of Giacomo da Lentini.* Translated by Richard Lansing. Toronto: University of Toronto, 2018. https://doi.org/10.3138/9781487518707.

Guinizzelli, Guido. *Rime.* Edited by Luciano Rossi. Turin: Einaudi, 2002.

Petrarca, Francesco. *Canzoniere.* Edited by Marco Santagata. Milan: Mondadori, 2018.

Petrarca, Francesco. *Petrarch's Lyric Poems: The* Rime sparse *and Other Lyrics.* Edited and translated by Robert M. Durling. Cambridge, MA: Harvard University Press, 1976.

Secondary Works

Balduino, Armando. *Boccaccio, Petrarca e altri poeti del Trecento.* Florence: Olschki, 1984.

Blanco Valdés, Carmen F. "Boccaccio y sus contemporáneos: Un debate poético." In *Parodia y debate metaliterarios en la Edad Media,* edited by Mercedes Brea, Esther Corral Díaz, and Miguel A. Pousada Cruz, 307–23. Alessandria: Edizioni dell'Orso, 2013.

Carrai, Stefano. "Esercizi petrarcheschi (con implicazioni cronologiche) del Boccaccio lirico." *Studi sul Boccaccio* 28 (2000): 185–97.

Cornish, Alison. *Vernacular Translation in Dante's Italy: Illiterate Literature.* Cambridge: Cambridge University Press, 2010. https://doi.org/10.1017/CBO9780511734762.

De Robertis, Domenico. "A norma di stemma (per il testo delle *Rime* di Boccaccio)." *Studi di filologia italiana* 42 (1984): 109–49.

Fedi, Roberto. "Pathways through the Lyric Forest (*Rime*)." In *Boccaccio: A Critical Guide to the Complete Works,* edited by Victoria Kirkham, Michael Sherberg, and Janet Levarie Smarr, 283–93. Chicago: University of Chicago Press, 2013.

Ferreri, Rosario. *Innovazione e tradizione nel Boccaccio.* Rome: Bulzoni, 1980.

Ferreri, Rosario. "Ovidio e *Le Rime* di G. Boccaccio." *Forum Italicum* 8, no. 1 (1974): 46–55. https://doi.org/10.1177/001458587400800103.

Ferreri, Rosario. "Sulle *Rime* del Boccaccio." *Studi sul Boccaccio* 8 (1974): 185–96.

Filosa, Elsa. *Boccaccio's Florence: Politics and People in His Life and Work.* Toronto: University of Toronto Press, 2022. https://doi.org/10.3138/9781487532727.

Gensini, Niccolò. "I classici nelle *Rime* di Boccaccio: Una proposta di lettura." In *Intorno a Boccaccio / Boccaccio e dintorni 2015*, edited by Stefano Zamponi, 15–26. Florence: Firenze University Press, 2016.

Kriesel, James C. *Boccaccio's Corpus: Allegory, Ethics, and Vernacularity*. Notre Dame, IN: University of Notre Dame Press, 2018. https://doi.org/10.2307/j.ctvpj7f5b.

Kumar, Akash. "Walls of Inclusivity: Dante's *Divine Comedy* and World Literature." In *A Companion to World Literature*, edited by Ken Seigneurie. West Sussex: John Wiley & Sons, 2020. https://doi.org/10.1002/9781118635193.ctwl0057.

Lanza, Antonio. "Boccaccio tardogottico: Pittura e poesia nelle *Rime*." In *Freschi e Minii del Due, Tre e Quattrocento: Saggi di letteratura italiana antica*, 105–20. Florence: Cadmo, 2002.

Lanza, Antonio. "Elementi di tradizione ed elementi d'innovazione nelle *Rime* del Boccaccio." In *Studi sulla lirica del Trecento*, 83–127. Rome: Bulzoni, 1978.

Lanza, Antonio. "Sulle *Rime* del Boccaccio: Ordinamento e Problemi di Attribuzione." In *Freschi e Minii del Due, Tre e Quattrocento: Saggi di letteratura italiana antica*, 91–104. Florence: Cadmo, 2002.

Machera, Virginia. "Per la biblioteca troiana di Giovanni Boccaccio: Il caso delle *Rime*." *Critica del testo* 23, no. 2 (2020): 61–81.

Natali, Giulia. "Il *Canzoniere* di Giovanni Boccaccio." *La Cultura* 39, no. 1 (April 2001): 55–92. https://doi.org/10.1403/12191.

Perella, Nicholas J. "Boccaccio's Lyric Poetry." *Italica* 38, no. 1 (March 1961): 1–14. https://doi.org/10.2307/477219.

Piccini, Daniele. "Le *Rime* del Boccaccio e la Bibbia." *Studi Ambrosiani di Italianistica* 4 (2014): 89–100.

Roncaglia, Aurelio. "Per le *Rime* di Giovanni Boccaccio: Appunti sulla critica e sul testo." *Annali della Scuola Normale Superiore di Pisa* 8, no. 4 (1939): 359–82. https://www.jstor.org/stable/24298950.

Sarteschi, Selene. "La poesia di Dante nelle *Rime* di Boccaccio." In *Autori e lettori di Boccaccio: Atti del Convegno internazionale di Certaldo: 20–22 settembre 2001*, edited by Michelangelo Picone, 289–326. Florence: Cesati, 2002.

Silber, Gordon R. *The Influence of Dante and Petrarch on Certain of Boccaccio's Lyrics*. Menasha, WI: George Banta, 1940.

Smarr, Janet Levarie. *Boccaccio and Fiammetta: The Narrator as Lover*. Urbana: University of Illinois Press, 1986.

Suitner, Franco. "Le rime di Boccaccio." In *Dante, Petrarca e altra poesia antica*, 211–42. Florence: Cadmo, 2005.

Suitner, Franco. "Sullo stile delle 'Rime' e sulle polemiche letterarie riflesse in alcuni sonetti." *Studi sul Boccaccio* 12 (1984): 3–10.

Tufano, Ilaria. "Forme e temi delle *Rime* di Boccaccio." In *Boccaccio in versi: Atti del Convegno di Parma, 13–14 marzo 2014*, edited by Pantalea Mazzitello,

Giulia Roboni, Paolo Rinoldi, and Carlo Varotti, 231–42. Florence: Franco Cesati, 2016.

Tufano, Ilaria. *"Quel dolce canto": Letture tematiche delle "Rime" di Boccaccio.* Florence: Franco Cesati, 2006.

Tusiani, Joseph. "The Poetry of Giovanni Boccaccio." *Thought* 50, no. 4 (December 1975): 339–50. https://doi.org/10.5840/thought197550431.

Usher, Jonathan. "*Quid referam Baias*: Boccaccio e il topos dei bagni." *Medioevo romanzo* 18 (1993): 105–14.

Vecchi Galli, Paola. *Padri: Petrarca e Boccaccio nella poesia del Trecento.* Rome: Antenore, 2012.

Weaver, Victoria. "The Apocryphal Boccaccio." *Mediaevalia* 34 (2013): 169–220. https://doi.org/10.1353/mdi.2013.0002.

Index of Italian First Lines

Lyrics by Boccaccio's correspondents are italicized.

Index of Names

THE LORENZO DA PONTE ITALIAN LIBRARY

General Editors: Luigi Ballerini and Gianluca Rizzo

Pellegrino Artusi, *Science in the Kitchen and the Art of Eating Well* (2003). Translated by Murtha Baca and Stephen Sartarelli. Introduction by Luigi Ballerini. Foreword by Michele Scicolone.

Lauro Martines, *An Italian Renaissance Sextet: Six Tales in Historical Context* (2004). Translated by Murtha Baca.

Aretino's Dialogues (2005). Translated by Raymond Rosenthal. Introduction by Margaret Rosenthal.

Aldo Palazzeschi, *A Tournament of Misfits: Tall Tales and Short* (2005). Translated by Nicolas J. Perella.

Carlo Cattaneo, *Civilization and Democracy: The Salvemini Anthology of Cattaneo's Writings* (2006). Edited and introduced by Carlo G. Lacaita and Filippo Sabetti. Translated by David Gibbons.

Benedetto Croce, *Breviary of Aesthetics: Four Lectures* (2007). Translated by Hiroko Fudemoto. Introduction by Remo Bodei.

Antonio Pigafetta, *The First Voyage around the World (1519–1522): An Account of Magellan's Expedition* (2007). Edited and introduced by Theodore J. Cachey Jr.

Raffaello Borghini, *Il Riposo* (2008). Edited and translated by Lloyd H. Ellis Jr.

Paolo Mantegazza, *The Physiology of Love and Other Writings* (2008). Edited with an introduction and notes by Nicoletta Pireddu. Translated by David Jacobson.

Renaissance Comedy: The Italian Masters, Volume 2 (2008). Edited with an introduction by Donald Beecher.

Renaissance Comedy: The Italian Masters, Volume 1 (2008). Edited with an introduction by Donald Beecher.

Cesare Beccaria, *On Crimes and Punishments and Other Writings* (2008). Edited by Aaron Thomas. Translated by Aaron Thomas and Jeremy Parzen. Foreword by Bryan Stevenson. Introduction by Alberto Burgio.

Leone Ebreo, *Dialogues of Love* (2009). Edited by Rossella Pescatori. Translated by Cosmos Damian Bacich and Rossella Pescatori.

Boccaccio's Expositions on Dante's Comedy (2009). Translated by Michael Papio.

My Muse Will Have a Story to Paint: Selected Prose of Ludovico Ariosto (2010). Translated with an introduction by Dennis Looney.

The Opera of Bartolomeo Scappi (1570): L'arte et prudenza d'un maestro cuoco (The Art and Craft of a Master Cook) (2011). Translated with commentary by Terence Scully.

Pirandello's Theatre of Living Masks: New Translations of Six Major Plays (2011). Translated by Umberto Mariani and Alice Gladstone Mariani.

From Kant to Croce: Modern Philosophy in Italy, 1800–1950 (2012). Edited and translated with an introduction by Brian Copenhaver and Rebecca Copenhaver.

Giovan Francesco Straparola, *The Pleasant Nights*, Volume 2 (2012). Edited with an introduction by Donald Beecher.

Giovan Francesco Straparola, *The Pleasant Nights*, Volume 1 (2012). Edited with an introduction by Donald Beecher.

Giovanni Botero, *On the Causes of the Greatness and Magnificence of Cities* (2012). Translated with an introduction by Geoffrey Symcox.

John Florio, *A Worlde of Wordes* (2013). A critical edition with an introduction by Hermann W. Haller.

Giordano Bruno, *On the Heroic Frenzies* (2013). A translation of *De gli eroici furori* by Ingrid D. Rowland. Edited by Eugenio Canone.

Alvise Cornaro, *Writings on the Sober Life: The Art and Grace of Living Long* (2014). Translated by Hiroko Fudemoto. Introduction by Marisa Milani. Foreword by Greg Critser.

Dante Alighieri, *Dante's Lyric Poetry: Poems of Youth and of the* Vita Nuova *(1283–1292)* (2014). Edited with a general introduction and introductory essays by Teodolinda Barolini. With new verse translations by Richard Lansing. Commentary translated into English by Andrew Frisardi.

Vincenzo Cuoco, *Historical Essay on the Neapolitan Revolution of 1799* (2014). Edited and introduced by Bruce Haddock and Filippo Sabetti. Translated by David Gibbons.

Vittore Branca, *Merchant Writers: Florentine Memoirs from the Middle Ages and Renaissance* (2015). Translated by Murtha Baca.

Carlo Goldoni, *Five Comedies* (2016). Edited by Gianluca Rizzo and Michael Hackett, with Brittany Asaro. With an introduction by Michael Hackett and an essay by Cesare de Michelis.

Those Who from Afar Look like Flies: An Anthology of Italian Poetry from Pasolini to the Present (2016). Edited by Luigi Ballerini and Beppe Cavatorta. Foreword by Marjorie Perloff.

Guittone d'Arezzo, *Selected Poems and Prose* (2017). Selected and translated with an introduction by Antonello Borra.

Giordano Bruno, *The Ash Wednesday Supper* (2018). A new translation of *La cena de le ceneri* with the Italian text annotated and introduced by Hilary Gatti.

Giacomo da Lentini, *The Complete Poetry* (2018). Translated and annotated by Richard Lansing. Introduction by Akash Kumar.

Remo Bodei, *Geometry of the Passions: Fear, Hope, Happiness: Philosophy and Political Use* (2018). Translated by Gianpiero W. Doebler.

Scipio Sighele, *The Criminal Crowd and Other Writings on Mass Society* (2018). Edited with an introduction and notes by Nicoletta Pireddu. Translated by Nicoletta Pireddu and Andrew Robbins. With a foreword by Tom Huhn.

Gasparo Contarini, *The Republic of Venice:* De magistratibus et republica Venetorum (2020). Edited and introduced by Filippo Sabetti. Translated by Giuseppe Pezzini with Amanda Murphy.

Donatien Alfonse François, Marquis de Sade, *Journey to Italy* (2020). Translated, introduced, and annotated by James A. Steintrager.

Scipio Slataper, *My Karst and My City* and Other Essays (2021). Edited, with an introduction and notes, by Elena Coda. Translated by Nicholas Benson and Elena Coda.

Federico Della Valle, *The Queen of Scots: La reina di Scotia* (2023). Translated by Fabio Battista.

Tusiani, *The Complete Poems of Michelangelo* (2023).

John Ruskin, *The Stones of Venice* (2025). Edited, with an Introduction and Notes, by William C. McKeown.

Vittorio Alfieri, *Life* (2025). Edited, translated, and annotated by Gianpiero W. Doebler. With an introduction by Giorgio Ficara.

Piero Gobetti, *An Intellectual Against Fascism: Selected Writings* (2025). Edited by Mimmo Cangiano, Davide Dalmas, Sandro-Angelo de Thomasis, and Marta Vicari. Translated by Sandro-Angelo de Thomasis.

Cesare Pavese, *The Craft of Living: Journals, 1935–1950* (2025). Edited, introduced, and annotated by Iuri Moscardi. Translated by Julian Sachs.

Those Who from Afar Look like Flies: An Anthology of Italian Poetry from Pasolini to the Present. Tome II, 1975–2015 (2025). Edited by Luigi Ballerini and Beppe Cavatorta. Foreword by Charles Bernstein.

Giovanni Boccaccio, *RIME: The Complete Lyric Poetry* (2025). Translation and Notes by Richard Lansing. Introduction by Akash Kumar.